Behavioral Family Therapy

Behavioral Family Therapy

An Evidence Based Approach

Bryan Crisp

MARRIAGE AND FAMILY THERAPIST, PRIVATE PRACTICE
GREENVILLE, NORTH CAROLINA

David Knox

PROFESSOR OF SOCIOLOGY
EAST CAROLINA UNIVERSITY

CAROLINA ACADEMIC PRESS
Durham, North Carolina

Library of Congress Cataloging in Publication Data

Crisp, Bryan.
  Behavioral family therapy : an evidence based approach / Bryan Crisp, David Knox.
      p. ; cm.
  ISBN 978-1-59460-627-4 (alk. paper)
  1. Family psychotherapy. 2. Behavior therapy. 3. Behavior therapy for children. I. Knox, David, 1943- II.
Title.
  [DNLM: 1. Family Therapy--Case Reports. 2. Behavior Therapy--Case Reports. WM 430.5.F2 C932b 2008]

  RC488.5.C75 2008
  616.89'156--dc22

                        2008041482

Carolina Academic Press
700 Kent Street
Durham, North Carolina 27701
Telephone (919) 489-7486
Fax (919) 493-5668
www.cap-press.com

Printed in the United States of America

To my parents, Earl and Betty Crisp, who were my first behavioral teachers. To my wife, Melynda, who has taught me the meaning of love. To my children, Mabel and Martha, who teach me daily that behavior is learned. And to Dr. Jeannie Golden, who taught me the details of behavioral analysis.

— Bryan Crisp

To Jack Turner and to Charles Madsen, the ultimate behaviorists in life and in therapy.

— David Knox

Contents

Preface

Accountability has become the focus of therapy. Parents and spouses in therapy want positive change for their money. This book delivers the goods. Rather than clients guessing about whether therapy is working, the increased frequency of positive behavior and the decreased frequency of negative behavior (along with the desired emotions/feelings) provide the answer.

Behavioral Family Therapy not only reviews the theoretical background for change but provides detailed, hands-on directives, scripts, and forms/charts for immediate use. It is the ultimate behavioral handbook for the therapist who treats families and marriages. Three chapters of case histories reveal both successes and failures, and leave no doubt about how to help parents and spouses achieve their family and marital goals.

Behavioral Family Therapy

Chapter 1

Behavioral Family Therapy: An Overview

People can use the principles of social learning theory to cope with everyday problems of family behavior management.

Gerald Patterson

A **behavioral approach** is the systematic application of learning principles to the management of human behavior. In behavioral family therapy, the therapist examines how family members learn undesirable behavior, how they can unlearn these behaviors, and how they can develop/learn more desirable behaviors. The book is not concerned with genetic or biochemical disorders such as autism, schizophrenia, and depression but with behavioral problems parents typically bring to therapy.

The behavioral therapist is concerned with certain relationships, principles, processes and resistances.

Relationships Behaviorists Focus On

The behavioral family therapist focuses on two sets of relationships: parent-child and husband-wife, in that order. By demonstrating to parents the effectiveness of behavioral procedures, parents become believers in the approach and knowledgeable about how it works, which can lead to working on one's marriage. However, sometimes working on the couple's marriage must precede working on family issues, since consistency of the parents is necessary to modify the behavior of children. In addition, being consistent in parenting requires spouses who enjoy and cooperate with each other.

Basic Assumptions/Principles

There are five basic assumptions/principles which underlie effective behavioral family therapy.

Behavior Is the Focus of Therapy

Children are not good or bad but small people who engage in behaviors that parents view as good or bad. Parents who complain that "my kids are driving me crazy" are asked to identify what their children DO that upsets them. Indeed, general complaints should be translated into specific behaviors to change.

Complaint of Parent	Behavioral Translation
"Selfish"	Low frequency of giving, sharing
"Mean"	High frequency of pushing/shoving/yelling at sibling
"Insolent"	High frequency of talking back/non-compliant behavior

Behavior Is Learned

Whatever children do which upsets parents has been learned, which can be understood on the basis of four rules of learning. We will define and give examples of each of these rules shortly.

Behavior Can Change

Whatever behaviors children have learned can be unlearned and new behaviors can be learned. Being polite can replace insolence, being compliant can replace resistance, and being helpful can replace being aloof and disinterested.

New Behavior Must Be Shaped

Shaping is the rewarding of successive approximations to the terminal goal. If the goal is for the child to come when called from another room, shaping would involve being with the child at the dinner table and asking him or her to "pass the salt." Since there is a very high probability the child would do what the parent asked in this context (pass the salt), the parent would set up other similar experiences. For example, at the end of a television program the child was watching, the parent might say, "It's time for bed; pick out your pajamas please." When the child did so, the parent would say, "Thank you for doing what mommy (or daddy, as the case may be) said." Gradually, the parent would increase the frequency of child compliant behavior and then spread the contexts in which the child is asked to do as the parent wishes. If the shaping has been frequent, and in small enough steps, the child will learn whatever the parent wants to teach.

The point for the parent is to set up positive learning experiences, reinforce small steps, and reinforce often. Constructing a context for a child to study involves beginning with studying for a few minutes a day and gradually increasing it. For the child who makes D's and F's, the child may not study at all. The parent will need to set aside time each day ,beginning with as few as five minutes and gradually increase to thirty minutes at a time, so that the child "learns to study." Of course, each "study segment" should be reinforced — followed by something pleasant (e.g. five minutes playing a video game).

A treatment program for thumb sucking provides yet another example of the importance of shaping. A child of five who sucks his thumb should gradually be reinforced for increasing amounts of time when he is not sucking his thumb. A minute is a safe beginning. The parent would say, *Brad, let's work together on helping you to stop sucking your thumb. I'm going to start the stop watch and if you cannot suck your thumb for a minute, you can put a check on this chart on the refrigerator. After you get ten checks, we will do something special with you like go to the toy store, go to the ice cream store, or rent a video.*

After the child earns the ten marks and gets the reinforcer, the parent will increase the amount of time necessary to get a reinforcer to five minutes, then to ten, etc. By taking small steps and increasing the steps slowly the child "wins" each time and keeps on winning. Over time, the child spends more and more time without sucking his thumb.

Of course, the parent would also verbally praise the child. For example, at the dinner table, the mother would tell the father, "Brad was a big boy today — he is learning not to suck his thumb and went for five minutes without doing so."

New Behavior Must Be Reinforced Immediately

Individuals learn most quickly when new behavior is reinforced. When children play quietly, are polite, and helpful (take their plate to the kitchen when a meal is over), it is important that parents reinforce them immediately. For example, when mother is preparing dinner in the kitchen and she hears her four- and five-year-old in the next room playing quietly, it is important that she stop washing the broccoli, dry her hands, and go into the next room and say, "Wow! How wonderful it is for you two to be playing so quietly." Similarly, when a child says "thank you" (exhibits polite behavior), the parent should make a big deal out of it — "you are a very polite little girl — you said thank you . . . your being polite is very nice and I am proud of you to be this way." And, when children display helpful behaviors, the parents should comment. When seven-year-old Tom notices that his dad dropped some lemons on his return from the grocery and picked them up for his dad, his dad should say, "I appreciate your helping me. You are a very helpful son."

Four Rules of Learning

As noted above, all behavior has been learned and can be explained on the basis of four rules of learning.

Reward Rule

The **reward rule** says that any behavior followed by a positive consequence will increase the frequency of that behavior. Whatever behaviors children engage in is a result of having been reinforced for those behaviors. Children who are polite, do as their parents ask, and clean their rooms have been reinforced for doing so. Children who do not come when they are called are being reinforced by the PlayStation they are playing, the TV program they are watching, or playing outside with their peers.

There are various types of reinforcers. These include primary (such as food), interpersonal (approval from parents), activities (watching TV, playing video games), and internal (the child self congratulates: "I am a good person" or "I did a good job."). **Tokens** are symbolic reinforcers and are used to bridge the gap between a primary reinforcer (e.g. ice cream) or activities (riding a go cart). Money is a token with which we are all familiar. A $20 bill is only print on paper but it can be exchanged for things we want and need (gas for the car, food, etc.) Later, we will show how tokens can be used to give children something NOW which they will trade in for something more tangible (e.g. ice cream, go cart ride, etc.).

Since rewarding behavior is very effective in getting behavior to recur, it is important that parents be aware that they sometime reward behavior they may not intend to. When a child tries to tie his or her shoes, sometimes the parent will brush his or her hands away and do it. In effect, the parent is not reinforcing "trying behavior" which leads to "independence." Ideally, the parent would be aware of the importance of the child being independent and reinforce the child for trying to tie his or her shoes and say "you are such a big girl (or boy) trying to do things for yourself." Not to reinforce independence is to teach a child to be helpless and dependent.

The reward rule can also be used to explain the development of negative behaviors such as hitting. A parent may complain that "Johnny has a real problem with hitting his sister and some of the kids at school." The reason Johnny hits is that it is instantly reinforcing. If he wants a video game from his sister and she says he can't have it, he simply hits her and takes it. If a peer at school has a book Johnny wants, he can get it quickly by shoving the guy and grabbing the book.

Negative Reinforcement Rule

The **negative reinforcement rule** says that any behavior associated with the termination of something negative will increase the frequency of that behavior. The buzz of an alarm clock is aversive. The ringing or buzz is stopped by the person pressing a button on the clock to turn it off. The act of pressing the button has been negatively reinforced since it ended the aversive sound.

The temper tantrum of a child is also aversive. Children use the principle of negative reinforcement to teach their parents to do what they want. For example, a child in the checkout line in the grocery store may grab a piece of candy. When the parent says "put that back" the child may begin to cry, drop to the floor, and yell. To stop this "scene" (a negative experience for the parent), the parent will say "OK" and give the child the candy. While the behavior of the parent (giving in to the child) can be explained by the negative reinforcement rule (the tantrum stopped), the behavior of the child (throwing a temper tantrum) can be explained by the reward rule (getting the candy).

Punishment Rule

The **punishment rule** states that any behavior followed by a negative consequence will decrease the frequency of that behavior. A child whose PlayStation is disconnected for a week when he or she does not come when called will be less likely to delay responding to a parent's request in the future. Punishers suppress behavior temporarily. When the highway patrol writes a speeding ticket, the driver will slow down until the patrol car is no longer in sight. Once the patrol car is gone, the driver may resume speeding. Similarly, a child who is slapped for sticking out his or her tongue to a parent will not do so in the presence of the parent. But when the parent leaves the room, the child may stick out his or her tongue at the parent again. Since punishers suppress rather than stop behavior, reinforcing behavior is more effective in creating and maintaining a desired behavior.

While punishment works, it is associated with negative outcomes. A parent who hits a child can stop the behavior of the child by doing so. But the child "models" on the parent and may hit his or her sibling as a way of controlling the sibling. Also, punishment begets punishment. Parents who yell and scream at their children discover that their children may yell and scream at them.

Extinction Rule

The **extinction rule** holds that any behavior which is consistently not reinforced will stop. Children who are never reinforced for asking for candy in the checkout line will stop asking. Parents who are never reinforced when they ask their children "how was your day?" will stop asking their children to interact. Above we noted the long term ineffectiveness of punishing a behavior and suggested that reinforcing the alternative behavior is preferable. For example, it may be more effective to reinforce the child for saying "please" and "thank you" by saying "you are very polite" than to punish the child for being impolite ("go to your room"). Extinction may be used in the same way. Rather than punish the child who does not say please, ignore it in combination with reinforcing the child when he or she is polite.

These four rules of learning represent the core of behavioral family therapy. While some behavior of children is innate (eye blink) or genetic (autism), for the most part, behavior is learned (and taught by parents). And, whatever negative behavior children have learned can be unlearned and new, more positive behavior can be learned (taught by parents).

The Nuts and Bolts of Behavioral Family Therapy

Some of the basics of behavioral family therapy include the following:

Baseline Data

A major distinction between a behavioral approach and other approaches is records. "If you can't count it, you can't change it" is the mantra of the behaviorist. Behaviorists do not guess about the frequency of a problem behavior or whether it is getting worse (increasing in frequency) or becoming less of a problem (decreasing in frequency). They count the behavior. Parents who complain "my child talks back all the time" are asked to count the frequency with which the child "talks back." By doing so, both parents and therapist will be able to evaluate the treatment program which should result in a decrease in talking back and an increase in polite behavior (defined as statements such as "thank you," "yes ma'am," etc.). Below is a Family Frequency Chart.

Family Frequency Chart

_____ (Name of Child)   Date: _____

_____ (Name of parent keeping records)

| | | | | Days of Week | | | |
Behaviors to Begin	Mon.	Tues.	Wed.	Thurs.	Fri.	Sat.	Sun.
1. _____	___	___	___	___	___	___	___
2. _____	___	___	___	___	___	___	___
3. _____	___	___	___	___	___	___	___
4. _____	___	___	___	___	___	___	___
5. _____	___	___	___	___	___	___	___

For example, if the parent complained, "my child never does what I ask," the therapist would define this as "noncompliant behavior" (meaning the child does not comply or do what the parent asks) and ask the parent to keep a record for one week of this behavior. If the parent asked the child to "turn off the TV" and the child kept watching TV, this would be one occasion of "noncompliance." If the parent asked the child to take out the trash and the child did not do so, this would be another example of noncompliance, etc. At the end of the day on Monday, if there were six occasions of noncompliance, the parent would write a six in the blank under Monday. The parent would keep similar records for noncompliant behavior on Tuesday and write a new number down for that day. Similarly, the parent may be concerned about other behaviors — talking back, arguing with siblings, leaving clothes in the living room — and would be keeping records on those behaviors as well.

The value of the parent keeping accurate records is that they keep the parents and therapist accurate about the frequency of the problem behavior and provide a way of evaluating the degree to which the intervention plan developed by the therapist is working. Parents who say "talking back isn't really a problem" may be surprised that it occurs eight times a day. Similarly, the therapist can only verify that the intervention is working by pointing to a dramatic drop in "talking back" (once every two weeks) and an increase in polite behavior (from zero to ten "thank yous" a week).

Each therapy session should end with giving the parent a Family Frequency Form (see Chapter 9) on which the parent is asked to keep a record of the behavior the parent wants their child to change. Each subsequent therapy session should begin with a review of the degree to which the behavior is increasing or decreasing.

There is no one way to keep a record of behavior. The Behavior Frequency Chart below is another way to chart behavior that provides a way to see a developing pattern. An example follows of the frequency with which Mark, a thirteen-year-old, either yelled or talked back to his mother. The mother simply recorded the frequency and returned it to the therapist.

Behavior Frequency Chart

Name: Mark
Behavior: Yelling or talking back to mother
Month and Week: September 8–14

	Monday	Tuesday	Wednesday	Thursday	Friday	Saturday	Sunday
10							
9							
8							
7							
6							
5						X	
4					X		
3		X					
2	X						
1			X				
0							X

Behavior Contracting

Once a baseline of the frequency of the behavior to change is identified, a contract is developed. Indeed, contracts are the core of behavioral family therapy. A **behavior contract** is an agreement which specifies who is to do what, when, and with what consequence. The content of a contract for young children (three to twelve) is developed by the therapist in consultation with the parents. Contracts with teenagers often involve input by the teenagers.

Contracts must be clear and behaviorally specific. A term like "clean room" is behaviorally defined as bed made, no clothes on floor, dirty clothes in laundry and closet door shut. Similarly, "studying" is defined as working five math problems, reading/talking to one's self about the content just read, or answering study questions in a room while the TV/music is off and the phone is not in use.

Contracts must include a consequence for the performance and nonperformance of the desirable behavior. Positive consequences are assigned for engaging in the desired behavior. The child who cleans his or her room as defined above gets to select from a menu of rewards such as watching TV, playing video games, staying up late, having friends over to spend the night, etc. Failure to engage in the desirable behavior is also assigned consequences, such as not being allowed to watch TV, etc.

In assigning consequences, it is important to select something that changes the behavior in the desired direction. We know if a consequence is a reward if, when it follows a behavior, it increases the frequency of the behavior. The focus is on the effect — if the behavior doesn't change in the desired direction, the consequence is not a reward. Similarly, a negative consequence or a punishment is only such when, if it follows a behavior, it decreases the frequency of the behavior. If a parent scolds their children for playing in the house and the children actually play more, the consequence of scolding was actually a "reward" (since playing behavior actually increased) not a punishment (since playing behavior did not decrease). The key elements of a behavior contract are behaviors and rewards as can be seen in the blank contract below. In addition, the contract specifies when the desirable behavior is to begin and for what period of time.

Family Behavior Contract

_____ (name of child) will _____ (desirable

behavior) beginning _____ (day of week) for _____ (days of week). For doing so, the

child will have earned the privilege to _____ (reward) and for not doing so,

will forfeit the reward.

If the parent complains that the child "doesn't do his homework," the therapist would fill out the contract as follows:

Family Behavior Contract

Mark (name of child) will *complete homework assignments* (desirable behavior) beginning *Monday at 4:15* for *Monday through Friday*. For doing so, the child will have earned the privilege to *watch TV and play video games* after dinner and for not doing so, will forfeit the reward.

Time Out as a Negative Consequence

While contracts are used most often for children ages 6 and over, an effective negative consequence for negative behavior of children age four and five is **time out** — or simply removing a child to a quiet room with no source of reinforcement (e.g. TV). A child who throws food at the table who is removed from the table and put in the bathroom for five minutes will usually decrease the frequency of food-throwing behavior.

Time out is a mild form of punishment that should be used early. A child who throws food should immediately be removed from the table and put in time out. Otherwise, there is the slow escalation of threats such as the parent saying "don't throw your food, honey" whereupon the child throws a roll, followed by the parent saying, "I told you not to throw your food," whereupon the child taunts the parent and flips a spoon on the floor, etc. The result is that the parent becomes enraged, slaps the child, and a jagged crying scene results with both parent and child upset. Had the parent removed the child immediately and put the child in time out when the child first threw food, the child would not have continued to do so and the situation would not have spun out of control.

Verbal Praise and Parental Consistency Are Essential

A key element of behavioral family therapy is to emphasize to parents the importance of "catching your child being good." Parents need to tell their child, "Thank you for waiting until mommy and daddy finished talking before asking your question," "You are polite to share your gum with me, thank you," and "You are a big girl to put your seat belt on by yourself." Sometimes the therapist will make an agreement with parents to ensure that they praise their children frequently.

Parent Agreement

Carol and John (parents of Mark) agree to *make two positive statements to Mark each day about something he did that pleased them* (desirable behavior).

Parental consistency is also paramount. Children are smart and they will learn what they are taught. If parents are not consistent, children will not change behavior consistently. For example, if parents want their child to take out the garbage and never praise their child for doing so or punish the child for not doing so (no computer games for next two days/nights) the child will not learn to take out the garbage. Rather, the child will depend on nagging from his or her parents as the stimulus for thinking about the garbage and only take out the garbage to stop the nagging (negative reinforcement). To help the child learn consistency, it is helpful for one parent to be responsible for the child management program and for the other parent to be in a supportive or backup role. However, both parents can engage in positive behavior toward the child, such as making two positive statements per day.

The Process of Therapy

The following details the behaviors of the behavioral family therapist from the first to the last session.

Building Rapport

Every therapist knows the importance of building **rapport** with his or her clients. This involves the high frequency use of reflective statements to the clients. "So, you feel frustrated that your child talks back and walks away when you ask him to do something." Such a statement by the therapist not only communicates empathy but allows the parents to correct the therapist if the statement is inaccurate (did the therapist get it right?). Parents feel favorably toward (have rapport with) a therapist they perceive as having empathy for their plight and who understands exactly what that plight is.

Having Parents Complete the Family Inventory

Chapter 9 features the **Family Inventory** which provides basic information the therapist needs to work with the parents. This can be completed with the parent or parents during the first session or mailed out ahead of time so that the parents bring it to the therapist the first meeting.

Defining Behaviors to Increase or Decrease

"What does your child do that upsets you?" is a key question to parents. This is followed by, "What would you like your child to do more often or to stop doing altogether?" These questions teach the parents to think behaviorally: from "my teenager is rebellious" to "my teenager leaves the house without telling me where he or she is going" to "I want my teen to ask me if he or she can go somewhere with friends and not talk back if I say no."

Explaining to Parents How the Behavior to Be Changed Has Been Learned

To provide the parents with an understanding of how the child's behavior has been learned, the therapist will identify antecedents to the child's behavior and the consequences that follow. It comes as no secret that the teenager who leaves the house without asking is avoiding being told that he or she cannot go. The larger problem is that the parents' approval has no value to the child so pleasing the parent does not process for the child. The therapist's goal is to get control of what the teen is and is not allowed to do by increasing the value of the parents' approval to the child. Once the teenager views the parent as an authority who controls rewards and punishments, the teen's behavior will be consistent with the parent's expectations.

Ranking Behaviors Parents Want Their Children to Change

After parents identify what new behaviors they would like their child to engage in (and have some understanding why their teenager does whatever he or she pleases), the therapist ranks the behaviors in terms of importance to the parents and focuses on one behavior. In effect, the therapist whittles down the plethora of "family problems" ("my kid is a wreck") to something manageable the parents can work on ("increasing study behavior"). By ranking and focusing on one behavior, the parents feel hope in getting a grip on their frustration and see a way to resolve it.

Identifying Rewards and Punishers as Consequences for Behavior

While parents may know what their child will work for in terms of ice cream, access to television, and being with friends as well as being denied these rewards, on occasion the child may be brought into therapy and asked to identify his or her own rewards. In general, the older the child (e.g. from twelve on), the more the therapist involves the child in family therapy. In effect, just as the therapist asks the parents what they want the child to do, the therapist may ask the child what he or she wants the parents to do.

Writing Up a Contract and Giving a Chart to Parents to Keep Records

A "behavior contract" (identified earlier) is drawn up to clarify what the child is expected to do, when, and with what consequence. Parents are also asked to keep records on the behavior they have identified that they wish their child to change so that both therapist and parents will know that the intervention is working. Below is an example of a form the therapist will give the parents to keep a record of the desirable behavior (see Chapter 9 for blank forms to give clients).

Frequency Chart

Mark (Name of Child)   Date: June 1–7
Mom (Parent keeping records)

Behavior to Begin	Mon.	Tues.	Wed.	Days of Week Thurs.	Fri.	Sat.	Sun.
1. *Complete homework assignments*	___	___	___	___	___	___	___

Consequence — Play video games

Discussing/Role Playing Implementation of Contract with the Child

Before parents leave the office, the therapist discusses what the parents are to say to the child. The parents should meet with the child together and say something like,

We have been concerned about some of the things going on in our family and are making some new rules. Study time is now going to happen before TV time or playing with friends in the afternoon. To make it easy to remember we have written down the new rules and will keep a record of when studying happens. We also want fun things to happen each day so that after studying, you can do something you like such as playing with friends, talking on the phone, or playing video games.

It is also helpful for the parents to say back to the therapist what the therapist said (role play) so that the therapist can give the parents feedback.

Resistances

While most parents "take to" a behavioral approach since it directly "gets at" what is bothering them (the child's behavior), there are resistances. Three complaints by parents that sometimes occur in reference to behavior therapy are:

"It Isn't Working"

Sometimes parents say that they are doing all the right things but nothing is working. The therapist will need to track each behavior the parent is engaging in and find out what the parent is not doing right. Since learning principles are like laws of gravity, if something isn't working, a learning principle is not being applied correctly. For example, a father said he tried to reinforce his daughter for studying but she "wasn't doing it right" so he got mad at her. In effect, the parent violated the principles of shaping.

Since the daughter had a baseline of zero time spent in studying and made all Ds the last reporting period, the behavioral goal was to make studying reinforcing by setting up initial short intervals of study time (fifteen minutes) and gradually increase the amount of time. In addition, the fact that she was sitting down to study was important to reinforce, so a focus on "did she work every math problem correctly?" is something that would follow later. The intervention plan went awry when the parent decided to make the daughter study for an hour at a time and then require everything she did to be perfect. In effect, an hour was too long for the daughter the first time out and having her father criticize her slow progress on her math problems further discouraged the daughter so that she shut down. The parent saying "the treatment doesn't work" was really revealing a violation of the principles of learning and shaping.

"It's Bribery"

Parents sometimes say "I'm not going to bribe my child to do what he or she should do anyway." **Bribery** is a legal concept whereby someone is offered money for doing something illegal. Paying someone to torch a building (commit arson) is bribery. There is nothing illegal about wanting a child to clean his or her room, study, or be polite. But positive consequences will determine whether or not the child learns these behaviors. Children need to learn two rules: "when I do good things, good things happen" and "when I do bad things, bad things happen." When children are rewarded for the desirable behavior and punished for the undesirable behavior, they behave consistent with the parents' expectations. Parents do not have a choice of whether or not there will be consequences for the behavior of their children. There WILL be consequences even if the parents do nothing (since doing nothing is a consequence). What is important is that the parents CHOOSE the consequences for the behavior of their children to affect the desired change. In effect, not to reward the child when the child does what the parent wants is to let the behavior extinguish (decrease in frequency). By rewarding the behavior, the child will continue and increase the behavior. The therapist might focus the parents on the behavior they want their child to engage in and encourage the parents to reinforce the behavior.

Aside from the illegal aspect of bribery, offering to give a child a big prize for a behavior must include shaping. A parent may say to a child, "If you make all A's, I'll buy you the Grand Theft Auto video game" or "Don't fight with your sister for a month and you can have someone over to spend the night." The problem with these promises is they do not break down into small sequences what is necessary to be successful. "Making all A's" requires daily concentrated study behavior and "not fighting with one's sister" requires daily vigilance to not be drawn into a fight and to learn an incompatible behavior. Hence, a parent who bribed a child to make A's or not fight would say that "I tried this reward thing and it doesn't work. I offered my kid a video game and a sleepover with a buddy and the kid still flunked out and fought with his sister." The behavioral therapist would point out that the fault lay in the faulty design of the behavior change program and that rewards do work.

"My Kid Should Do as I Say"

Parents feel that children should respect their authority and do as they are told. Children who respect authority have been taught to do so. By rewarding the child for doing what the parent wants him or her to do and punishing him or her for noncompliance, both the child and parent win. The child wins by learning to respect authority (today it is the parents, tomorrow it is the teacher, police officer, and warden). The parent wins by living with an obedient child in a family context that is not fraught with yelling and screaming.

Chapter 2

Assessment and Behavior Contracts

If you can't count it, you can't change it.

Charles Madsen

Effective family therapy depends on assessing the nature and frequency of the problems parents present in therapy and developing behavior contracts to ensure the desired behavioral change. In this chapter, we discuss each of these phenomena and provide examples.

Parents differ in their ability to identify for the therapist what their children are doing that upsets them. While some have a vague notion that something "isn't right," others know exactly what behaviors are troubling them. In either case, the therapist who conducts a thorough assessment will have a better shot at helping the family achieve their goals no matter how diffuse or specific the initial presentation by the parents.

Importance of Rapport during Assessment

Establishing rapport during assessment is as important as the assessment itself. The therapist should make reflective statements to each parent as he or she identifies what he or she views as "the problem." These reflective statements by the therapist such as "You become angry when your child talks back to you and feel that this disrespect is unacceptable" may also be accompanied by positive labeling such as "It is clear that you are caring and loving parents and that you want the best for your child." The therapist should make both sets of statements at a high frequency to help ensure a high level of rapport.

Such reflective affirmations are important since the parents may feel as if they are the "problem," that they should have handled things differently, and that their family is a mess because of them. Indeed, parents often present to the therapist that they are both defeated and tired. Some parents feel they have lost their ability to influence their child's behavior, that all of their beliefs about what constitutes good parenting are wrong, and that they are the object of failure from disapproving family and friends. These negative feelings and experiences of parenting may actually serve as a source of motivation for the parent — they want to end their distress of watching their child engage in destructive and nonproductive behavior and they seek answers in regard to how they can reverse the problem. In effect, therapy may be become a negative reinforcer in that it serves to remove the aversive feelings of failure and hopelessness.

Since most parents have no history of being in therapy, it is important for the therapist to make the first session as reinforcing as possible. Compiling assessment data takes both time and effort on the part of parents. Hence, the therapist is careful not only to avoid blaming them for the plight of their situation but to provide hope for resolving the problems they are having with their children. By reinforcing the parents for keeping records, the parents are more likely to do so which will be helpful in monitoring the progress of therapy. When parents can "see" behavioral charts that show a decrease in negative behavior and an increase in positive behavior, their motivation for therapy increases.

Stages of Assessment

Therapy proceeds through a series of specific stages.

Initial Questions

The behavior therapist begins the assessment during the first interview by asking a generic question such as, "What is happening in your family that concerns you?" Parents are invited to identify whatever concerns they experience. Subtleties in the actions of the family members may be noted such as who talks first (e.g. the more dominant partner), who talks the least or is silent (e.g. the more passive parent), and who interrupts whom (e.g. the more controlling parent).

Assessment begins by asking the parent or parents to describe their situation. If the mother says "my child wets the bed," she will be asked how often it occurs, and how she, her husband and child feel about it. It is also helpful to know when the behavior does and does not occur. "Under what conditions does your daughter have a 'dry' night? For those nights she remained dry, what was different (e.g. bedtime, amount of liquid before bed, etc.) from 'wet' nights?" Also, the therapist will want to know how the parents respond to the child who has a "wet" night (e.g. ignore, disgust, disapproval). And how do they respond to a "dry" night (e.g. ignore, approval, what)? The answer to these questions provides the therapist with what the child is doing which upsets them, when/how often the behavior occurs, and what they say or do to the child after the behavior occurs. The latter helps the therapist to know in what way parents are reinforcing the undesirable behavior and punishing the desirable behavior.

History of Previous Interventions

By the time parents seek professional help, they have exhausted their resources for ways to change the problem behavior. Typically, parents, neighbors, friends, and teachers have all been asked how to resolve the problem behaviors. Asking the parent or parents in therapy whom they have previously consulted will give the therapist an idea of the family's social environment and whom they regard as resources when problems arise. It is helpful to know these resources for two reasons. First, these individuals are often seen as "experts" by the family and may have a high reinforcement value. The therapist may decide to utilize these people in the upcoming behavioral intervention. Second, by knowing what has not worked, the therapist may be sure the suggested intervention is new.

ABC (Antecedents, Behaviors, and Consequences) Records

After building rapport and getting initial information, the clinician introduces the **ABC form** which provides a method of recording antecedents, behaviors and consequences of the "problem" behavior (see example below).

Date: 5/5/09   Time of Day: 9:23 PM

1. What behavior did you see? (circle all that apply)

__ fighting   __ running away   __ breaks things   __ tantrum

__ refusing to follow rules (describe) _____

__ aggression (describe) _____

__ crying

__ other (describe) _____

2. What was going on when the behavior occurred?

__ school work (what?)_____

__ asked to do something (what? *e.g. go to sleep in one's own bed*)

__ asked not to do something (what? *e.g. don't mark on wall*)

__ told to stop doing something (what? *e.g. turn off TV*)

3. Who was around when the behavior started? (circle)

__ mom __ dad __ sister __ brother __ teacher __ classmates __ people in store

__ other_____

4. Where was the child when the behavior started? (circle)

__ outside __ classroom __ kitchen __ bedroom __ living room __ in car

__ grocery store __ shopping __ restaurant

__ other (where?) _____

5. What happened after the child engaged in the behavior? (circle)

__ taken from the room __ spanked __ sat in time out __ spoken to __ left alone

__ grounded __ hugged

__ other (describe:_____)

Parents are instructed to complete the form each time any behavior occurs. Following a behavior, the parent completes the time and day and simply circles where, when, and what happened before, during, and after the behavior.

Parental Reaction to Record Keeping Request

Parents sometimes feel overwhelmed with the number of problem behaviors: bed wetting, tantrums, talking back, whining, and fighting. The clinician should help the parents to prioritize the behaviors they want to work on and work from the top down. By initially focusing on one behavior, the parents are less likely to feel overwhelmed. With each new success, the parents move down the list to the next problem behavior. Of course, each success increases the motivation of the parents to work on other behaviors.

Reviewing ABC Reports with Parents

The therapist reviews with the parents the ABC forms they provide by looking for trends and patterns. Some behaviors will simply be age-appropriate for a child (e.g. tantrums for a three-year-old). Others behaviors will be identified as worthy of concern (e.g. destruction of property or self-injury). Behaviors that involve bodily harm to the child or pose a danger to others must be dealt with immediately (e.g. fire setting or playing with matches).

After dangerous and destructive behaviors are addressed, others may become the focus of therapy. Parents may surprise the therapist in what they identify as top priorities. For example, some parents are more concerned with whining than the child's tantrums. Whatever behaviors they identify to change, the ABC forms are helpful to the therapist to begin an intervention program.

Consider the case of Allison, a five-year-old girl who cried when she was put to bed. To get Allison to stop crying, her mother and father (before they came to therapy) took turns lying in bed with Allison until she fell asleep. On several occasions, the mother or father also fell asleep and did not awaken for several hours. The drawbacks of this strategy were that it not only resulted in Allison's being dependent on them to fall asleep, but the couple missed spending time with each other at the end of the day.

When Allison's parents returned the ABC report, the therapist noted their concern about Allison's crying and thrashing in the bed at bedtime and expressed the desired behavioral goal in positive terms: Allison's laying in bed alone without crying until she fell asleep. Once this goal was identified, a behavior contract was negotiated between Allison and her parents.

Using Behavior Contracts

In order to develop an effective behavior contract, the therapist must identify what rewards or reinforcers can be used to affect the desired behavior. One of Allison's favorite children's programs ("Singing with Sally Salamander") comes on in the morning as she is getting ready for preschool. She enjoys watching the characters dance and sing and sometimes she will dance and sing along with them. In a behavior contract, parents offer a preferred item or activity the child enjoys in exchange for the child's appropriate behavior. In this case, Allison agrees to lie in bed quietly without her parents until she falls asleep. When she does, she will earn the right to watch her favorite morning program as she gets ready for preschool (see below).

Allison's Agreement

At bedtime, Allison will lie in the bed by herself without crying, until she falls asleep. For doing so, she will earn the right to watch "Singing with Sally Salamander" in the morning as she gets ready for school. If she cries when she goes to bed or wants mother or daddy to lay down with her, she loses the right to watch "Singing with Sally Salamander" in the morning. She will have the opportunity to try again the following night.

Signed this day of 5/5/08:

Allison Brown _____Mother and Daddy _____

There are several important elements to the contract with Allison. First, it defines what Allison must do (go to bed by herself without crying). Second, it identifies the reward for successful completion of the behavior (she will earn the right to watch "Singing with Sally Salamander" while getting ready for school the next day). Third, it describes what will happen when the behavior does not occur (she will lose the privilege to watch "Sally Salamander"). Fourth, the contract notes that if the desired behavior does not occur, Allison will have the opportunity to try again the following night. This is important since the child learns that he or she will have another chance at performing the correct behavior and gaining the desired reward.

Asking the child what she or he would like to earn as a reward can increase the child's motivation to do what the parents want. In the absence of the child telling the therapist what they want, the therapist may look at the child's high frequency behaviors. Allison watched "Sally Salamander" EVERY MORNING and it was her preferred DVD, so the therapist can be assured that this is a reinforcer.

An important consideration in developing a behavior contract is to keep the contract simple so that the child will have a high chance of success. "Go to bed alone and don't cry and you get Sally Salamander" is clear and simple. The therapist may engage the child in other ways such as encouraging the parents to let the child decorate or color the contract with them. The child may also draw pictures of herself lying in bed with a smile on her face with parents in another room of the house. Children sometimes enjoy being creative, which increases their motivation and compliance.

Manage the Environment via Antecedents

The intervention described above provides a positive consequence in exchange for the desired behavior. Another strategy to effect the desired behavior is to manage the environment or change antecedent conditions. Suppose the ABC report showed that Allison is put to bed at 8:30 some nights and other nights at 9:30 or 10:00. An antecedent intervention would be to inform parents of the age-appropriate bedtime for their child . . . in this case the therapist asks the parents to consider 8:15 as the regular bedtime for Allison. Bedtime routines can be identified as follows: Allison takes a bath from 7:30 until 8:00, puts on her pajamas, brushes her teeth and climbs into bed by 8:15. She may pick out her favorite stuffed animal to sleep with and mom or dad will read to her until 8:30, at which time her parents will kiss her good night and leave the room.

A separate behavior contract was made with Allison's parents whereby they agreed to begin Allison's bedtime routine at 7:30 with her ending up in the bed at 8:15. Sometimes, only a verbal agreement is made. In effect, two new events are to take place in the family — Allison's new bedtime is 8:15 (managing the environment via a new antecedent) and she is rewarded (via a contract) each morning for not crying when the parents leave the room (8:30). By using antecedent as well as consequences, Allison's chance of engaging in the new behavior is increased.

Follow-Up Record Keeping

The therapist and parents will know if the intervention plan is working only if accurate records are kept. In effect, we won't know if Allison is lying in bed alone without crying each night unless her parents keep records. The Time Frequency Chart is helpful to track a behavior once it has been defined and an intervention has been planned. To use this form, parents only have to mark a box when the desired behavior occurs. In this case a capital B (for Behavior) was agreed upon for parents to show the time Allison was put to bed without crying. An abridged version of the chart is presented below. An expanded version is presented in Chapter 9, Family Therapy Forms.

Child: Allison   Put the letter of the code in the box at the time it occurs.
Record keeper: Mom or Dad   I will ask for this sheet every time we meet for therapy.
Behavior: Alone in bed   An empty box means no behavior occurred.
                No crying
Week of: 5/5/08–5/12/08   **B = alone in bed, no crying**

	Mon	Tues	Wed	Thurs	Fri	Sat	Sun
7:00 PM							
7:30 PM							
8:00 PM							
8:30 PM				B	B		
9:00 PM							

Allison's behavior is noted as "Behavior." "Record Keepers" are Allison's mother or father. The week being tracked is indicated in the space provided. Parents will notice directions on the form pertaining to its completion as well as directions for its return to the therapist. The clinician should use a sample form to demonstrate how the behaviors are indicated. The therapist may say, "Suppose Allison follows the contract and goes to bed at 8:30 without either of you having to stay in bed with her. When this is the case, you will write the letter B in the 8:30 box. This way, I will know she went to bed that night without crying. If, on the other hand, she cried when she went to bed and you had to lie next to her until she fell asleep, you write nothing in the box and I will know that the behavior did not happen."

In the example, Allison went to bed on Thursday and Friday nights alone and without crying. The following mornings, she was allowed to watch "Sally the Singing Salamander." However, the previous days she cried when alone so that her parents lay in bed with her and stayed until she fell asleep. The following mornings Allison was not allowed to watch television, but was reminded that tonight she may go to bed without crying to earn this privilege the next day.

User Friendly Charts

Both the ABC and Time Frequency Chart are designed so that parents can quickly mark if the desired behavior occurred. When the therapist explains the record keeping chart to the parents, he or she should emphasize the importance of keeping the chart up to date and marking it soon after the desired behavior. If parents want to provide more in-depth information, they may do so; however, if these items and boxes are checked, the clinician will have enough information to be helpful. Similarly, if the therapist wants to understand a particular night or event, he or she need only ask the parents for details.

Praise for Parents

Data collection is one of the most difficult challenges behavior therapists encounter. Parents are not accustomed to keeping records and some may resist doing so. Viewing record keeping as a behavior and being aware that any behavior that is reinforced will continue, the behavior therapist makes it a point to praise the parents for keeping records and being consistent with delivering consequences (in this case making sure that Allison sees "Sally Salamander" only following a night she goes to bed alone and does not cry). Specific statements by the therapist might include "I can tell that you are a good parent because you work hard to give me the information I need to help you," "You did a wonderful job keeping and bringing in these records," and "I know it wasn't easy to deny Allison "Sally Salamander" the morning following a night that she cried."

Asking for reports at the beginning of the session will also enhance the chance that data collection occurs. If parents learn that the therapist will ask for the completed forms at the beginning of each therapy session, they will come to expect the request and are more likely to keep and bring data sheets to the therapist. A request for cooperation from parents would sound like, "I cannot be there to see your child do these things, so in order for me to be the most helpful for you, I need for you to complete and bring in these forms. I will ask for them at the beginning of each session. OK?"

When Parents Provide No Records

What happens when parents do not keep records and/or show up without them? Just as the contract between the child and the parents allows for "some slack," the implicit agreement between the therapist and the parents should allow for times when data collection was not completed. "I'm glad you are here today and I know we can help your daughter. Will you be sure to remember to bring the forms back with you at the next session?" Parents may still be able to name instances of problem behavior during the previous week. Although this type of delayed recording is error-prone, it is sometimes better than no report and no data.

In addition to making requests for forms to be turned in, the therapist should also ask if parents have questions about how the forms are to be completed. The charts and forms may make plenty of sense while parents are sitting with the therapist, but upon their return home parents may feel confused when interactions with the child begin.

It is not unusual for parents to feel embarrassed to admit that these behaviors (e.g. child cried all week and never wanted to be alone) have occurred. Some parents have admitted that they feel guilty when recording the behavior sequence because they may realize how their actions contribute to the child's misbehavior. It is desirable for parents to gain knowledge of their own behavior and parents need to be reassured that they are also learning, just like the therapist and like the child. The therapist should emphasize that these reports are to help their family work better together. It is impossible to know what is happening without good information and they should be congratulated for taking good data for the therapist.

Other parents will ask if they may fax or mail forms to the therapist when complete. Take them up on it. While getting the data in the office is preferable, mailed or faxed data is still data.

Maintaining Behavior Change

Over a series of sessions, the therapist monitors the return of records and reinforces parents for their hard work. After the behavior has continued for a reasonable period of time, the reinforcers can be faded. It is the final step of behavioral intervention to fade the consequences so that the behavior becomes more self-sustaining. In behavioral terms this means that Allison will shift from going to bed without crying because she can watch "Sally the Salamander" the next day to going to bed without crying since she feels "independent" and "good about herself'" when she does so. In effect she shifts from an "external" to an "internal/cognitive" reinforcer.

In our example, Allison begins to sleep alone without crying each night. Her parents continue to record Allison's behavior each night until finally, the child has learned to go to sleep alone and not cry. Parents, however, should continue the antecedent part of the program such as making 8:30 PM Allison's bedtime. And, they can routinely put on "Sally Salamander" in the morning. Of course, the parents would continue to verbally praise Allison. "You are such a big girl sleeping in your own bed without mommy or daddy. We are sssssoooooo proud of you."

Other behaviors will require more planning to maintain and to generalize them. Steven is a five-year-old boy who wets his pants at school. From ABC reports submitted by his teacher and parents, the therapist learned that when Steven wets his pants, classroom activity stops. Teachers and classmates focus their attention on Steven. And, because there is no change of clothes at school, his parents are called and Steven is taken home.

Because Steven's behavior is reinforced in several ways (attention from teachers, attention from classmates, escape from school to home where he plays video games, etc.) a new strategy was developed to decrease "wetting accidents." The new consequence for Steven being dry up to 11:00 AM was that his mother would come and get him and take him home. However, it was clear from the beginning that Steven's parents could not continue to pick Steven up from school indefinitely which required a systematic fading program as follows:

The behavior intervention began with Steven being picked up each day for a week when his clothes were dry at 11:00 AM. Before leaving the classroom, Steven was also given the opportunity to say a poem, sing a song, share some work he had done or share a preferred item with the class. The next week, he was picked up at 11:00 every other day when his pants were dry. Additionally, on the days he was not picked up (when he is dry), his parents were called at work and he was allowed to tell them that he had been dry that day. He was also allowed to tell the class a story or share a special item with the class on all dry days.

On the third week, his parents picked him up once per week if he was dry at 11:00 and each day he was dry he was allowed to share some of his work, sing a song or tell a story to the class. Finally, Steven's parents picked him up from school every now and then until, gradually, Steven stayed at school and was dry all day. Teachers also participated in the fading program by allowing Steven to share items and tell stories the first week he was dry and then fading his doing so over time so that wetting no longer occurred.

When behavior interventions and contracts are made, it is a good idea to begin with an idea of how the intervention will be faded. In this case, parents are reassured that they would not have to pick up their child from preschool every day for the remainder of the year. Initially, the parents' picking up Steven every day was a major reinforcer and contributed to his staying dry. Over several weeks the mother's picking him up as a reinforcer was faded as other reinforcers were put in place — sharing his work and being "on stage" in his classroom.

Chapter 3

Young Children: Problems and Solutions

Find out what a child will work for, and what a child will work to avoid, systematically manipulate these contingencies and you can change the behavior of the child.

Jack Turner

Parents come to family therapy because their child is engaging in behavior which is upsetting to them. In this chapter, we look at typical problems parents present for children ages two through eleven. In Chapter 5, we discuss problems related to teenagers (ages 12–18).

Being Aware of Age-Stage Development

Parents may benefit from having some basic information about child development. For example, Ethan (age four) may cry at the kitchen table when he perceives that his sister Mary (age six) has a tall glass of juice compared to his glass, which is wider but shorter. Although the liquid in each glass is the same, the child has not mastered the developmental task of **conservation of mass** and believes he has less juice. Parents, knowing this principle, would understand Ethan's view and recognize that he needs time to mature so as to develop new cognitive skills.

In addition to conservation of mass, another principle parents might be aware of in young children is that of **egocentricity** which denotes that children can see the world from only one point of view — their own. At Nicholas's (age five) birthday party, Bobby (age four) becomes angry and runs off with the locomotive of Nicholas's new toy train. When reprimanded by his parents and made to return the locomotive, Bobby cries. His mother feels embarrassed at her child's behavior. However, she is reassured by the therapist who informs her that three- to five-year-olds are often egocentric in their behavior. Knowing this principle helps his mother structure Bobby's surroundings so there is less chance for his behavior to become a problem. For instance, she might have Bobby sit further away from the opening of presents, reward him for playing with another object before the present is opened, and teach him appropriate behavior by encouraging Bobby to clap his hands when Nicholas opens his presents. Parents might consider that it may be more desirable to teach Bobby what to do when presents are being opened instead of reprimanding him when he does what is normal for a three- to five-year-old.

Keeping the Child Safe

Childhood can be an exciting time of new discoveries. As the child matures, the child has new ideas and discovers new abilities he or she did not know that he or she had. It seems children become little scientists as they test their new skills and abilities. Parents sometimes have difficulty staying ahead of their children as the children test their abilities and the environment. For example, the crawling baby will soon be walking and putting a variety of objects in his or her mouth. Whether the child is motivated by the desire to understand the texture of an item, to ease teething pain, or to satisfy an urge to taste and consume the object, parents will need to be alert to keep their child safe. One two-year-old inadvertently found some of her parents' pills and ate them as though they were candy. When the mother discovered the child eating the pills, she called the pediatrician who informed her "meet me in the emergency room immediately since we must pump the child's stomach." Parental vigilance of young children must never relax.

A major role of parents is to socialize their children so that they can be productive members of society. The role involves teaching their children early that they must follow rules. This implies obedience to parents who set the rules. For example, the five-year-old child who is riding a bike for the first time may be feel exuberant (reinforced by bike riding) while peddling down the block and want to keep going. Much to her mother's surprise, the child turns the corner and is no longer visible which prompts the mother to institute a new rule about biking distance. Hence, as children test their abilities, parents will need to set limits to keep them safe.

Letting the Child Learn Natural Consequences

Just as parents need to set rules to keep children safe, they must also allow their children freedom to experience their own mistakes and to learn how to deal with the consequences of their own actions. The child's learning must occur under the parents' supervision. When the child is allowed to play with a kite on a day that is very windy, the child learns why it is not a good idea to fly a kite on a day that is too windy. In this case, losing the kite may be difficult enough for the child without the parent having to reprimand the child for the same thing. Parents will only have to help the child "connect the dots" between their actions and the consequence. The parent may calmly say, "I know you are sad that the kite blew away and you now understand why it is best to pick a day without wind gusts to fly a kite." In effect, the parent let the child fly the kite on a windy day to discover the natural consequence of losing the kite so that the child may be more selective in choosing when to fly a kite.

Being Consistent with Consequences

Mary Sue's parents have taught her to put her dirty dishes in the sink after she finishes dinner. For three months Mary Sue has carried her dishes from the table to the kitchen after she finished her supper. After doing so, she was allowed to eat dessert. One night Mary Sue finished her supper and asked for dessert before she had taken her plate to the kitchen. Her parents noticed that the table had not been cleared and wondered, "What is going on?" From a behavioral perspective, the child is developing a sense of independence and is testing the rule to see if it still applies. If her parents let her have dessert without clearing the table, Mary will learn that she no longer needs to clean the table.

By reaffirming for Mary Sue that dessert follows putting her dishes in the sink, the parents send the message that the rule has not changed so that Mary Sue will be less likely to test this rule in the future. Parental consistency in rules is important since it teaches children not to continually test the rules. Parents who complain, "My child never listens to me and doesn't do what I say" have simply not been consistent in enforcing rules with the child. In effect, the child has learned, "I can do what I want since there are no rules. One day my parents enforce a rule and the next day they don't. So I will assume that I am always on a day where they won't apply consequences." Once children learn that there are no rules, parents will begin a daily nightmare since their children will be completely out of control — they'll come to dinner when they want, eat what they want, get up when they want, leave the house when they want, come home when they want, etc.

Changing Rules as the Child Gets Older

Parents will need to change rules as the child gets older. A child who is ten should have rules that are different from a child who is six. For example, bedtime for a ten-year-old might be 9:00 PM while bedtime for a six-year-old will be closer to 7:30 PM.

While parental boundaries and rules should change to accommodate children as they grow and change, parents often wonder the difference between when a child is simply testing the rules and when the child needs new rules that take into account a more advanced maturational level. In regard to age and bedtime, the older the child, the later the child's bedtime.

The therapist and parents should discuss what rules the parents have established and how the rules are working. If Martha's bedtime is 9:00 or 9:30 and she is irritable the next morning, it may be a good idea for the parents to set her bedtime back to 8:30 or 8:00 and assess the effect on her irritability the next morning. Each child is different and Martha may need an earlier bedtime than her peers.

Identifying Values and Setting Up House Rules

Parents will need to decide what values they want their children to have and identify what behavioral rules reflect these values. John and Mary identified the following values/rules for Brittany, their six-year-old:

1. Value — politeness. Rule — family members say "please," "thank you, and "excuse me."

2. Value — soft voices. Rule — family members use "inside voices" when inside the house. "Inside voices" refers to family members speaking in a low volume when inside the house.

3. Value — safety. Rule — family members walk and do not run in the house.

4. Value — clean floors. Rule — family members take off their shoes when entering the house.

5. Value — save money. Rule — family members turn off lights after leaving a room.

It is a good idea for the therapist to guide the initial rule-setting process. The therapist should ask the parents to identify the values they want their children to adopt and the behaviors associated with those values. Consistent with the principle of shaping discussed earlier, parents should initially focus on no more than three values and rules for a young child to follow. Six-year-olds can handle four to five rules; an eight-year-old child can have as many as ten. Each child is different, but it is preferable to begin with too few rules rather than too many. In many cases, the therapist will be formalizing rules that have never been stated, so it is best that the number of rules remain low in the beginning. As parents see their child following and conforming to the rules, they can gradually increase the number.

After the values have been identified, the associated behavioral rules should be stated in positive behavioral terms. Children are asked to "use soft voices" rather than "don't yell," to "walk slowly" rather than "don't run," and to say "thank you" rather than grab something and say nothing. These expectations identify what is expected and invite the children to comply.

Encouraging Parent-Child Collaboration on House Rules

Children are more likely to comply with house rules when they are asked by their parents to collaborate in setting them up. In addition to parents identifying certain house rules, they may invite their children to suggest others. Parents may also discuss the reasons why rules are important and enlist the aid of the children in setting up appropriate consequences. For example, the value of having clean floors may result in the behavior of taking one's shoes off when entering the house. The person who tracks in mud or forgets to take off his or her shoes would forfeit the right to watch TV that evening. And this house rule would apply to parents as well as the children. So if daddy forgets to take off his shoes, his children may remind him that he can't watch the evening news.

Involvement of the children can also be expressed by their converting the list of "House Rules" to a poster or bulletin board that they decorate with their favorite characters. The list can also be ceremoniously placed in an area visible to all — the refrigerator is a favorite. A by-product of getting the children involved in the development, write-up, and placement of the "House Rules" is that they become keenly aware of what the house rules are and are not surprised when parents remind them that "walking" in the house is one of the house rules.

As noted earlier in Chapter 1, new behaviors can be established more quickly when they are reinforced. This means that the parents should be alert to their children following the house rules and promise their children. When children say "thank you," take their shoes off when entering the house, and turn off the lights when leaving a room, the parents should shower them with praise with phrases such as "you are very polite," "thanks for keeping the floor clean," and "you are great to help the family save money by turning off the lights so that we can spend the money doing family fun things." Behavior that is reinforced will continue. Behavior that is ignored will eventually stop.

An example from the Bragg family illustrates how house rules work on a daily basis. Kelly is seven and recently helped her parents think up and post her family's "House Rules." One day, Kelly's dad walked into the family room where Kelly was playing and asked her to choose between juice and milk to drink with dinner. Kelly responded, "I would like milk please." (Saying "please" reflects that Kelly is following the house rules of being polite.) Her father noticed her response and said, "Kelly, great job! I see that you are being polite which is one of the house rules! That's wonderful, thank you!" The father's reinforcement let Kelly know that she had followed the "House Rules," that her dad had noticed her doing so, and that he had praised her for her compliance. Consistent with the "reward rule," Kelly will likely continue to be polite.

Alerting Parents to "Catch Their Children Being Good"

It is easy to miss all of the times children follow rules. To be effective in getting children to do what the parents want, parents need to be attentive to their child's behavior. Children are constantly following rules and complying with directions. Parents need to know what behaviors to watch for and then reinforce the child when he or she engages in the desired behavior.

Not attending to desired behavior is what normally occurs. As family members interact and go about their daily routines, there is little reinforcement for parents to pay attention, for example, to children playing quietly or speaking softly. Only when siblings are heard arguing and yelling in the next room do parents notice. The point for parents is to "catch their children being good." In effect, the parent or parents would go into the room where the siblings are playing quietly and, using soft voices, say, "How wonderful that you two are playing together so nicely and so softly. Wanna go get some ice cream?" Such behavior on the part of the parent or parents helps to reinforce/lock in the behavior parents want their children to engage in.

Alternatively, if parents only attend to their children when they are doing something wrong like fighting in the next room, they (the parents) may inadvertently be reinforcing the negative behavior by giving it attention. So, without awareness, parents may be reinforcing and teaching children to engage in the very behavior they do not want.

The following is an example of how a parent "caught her children being good" and doing so had an immediate positive effect. Jennifer and Dan were eight- and eleven-year-old stepsiblings. Christy, their mother, came to therapy complaining that fights were common as Jennifer and Dan picked on each other relentlessly. House rules were established such that the value was "getting along" and the behavior was "playing quietly" (not fighting). The goal in therapy was for the parents, Christy and her husband, to encourage Jennifer and Dan to play quietly and not fight.

Christy recounted a typical day. She would pick up Jennifer and Dan from school in the afternoon. After returning home, the kids would have a snack and begin their homework. Christy explained to the therapist that sibling fights would begin in the car as the children told her about their respective day, each interrupting the other. The fighting would continue all the way home and inside the house. The scenario was that the kids would pick at each other while Christy was in the role of the referee.

The therapist asked Christy to be vigilant for and verbally reinforce Jennifer and Dan when they were *not* fighting. The next day, on the way home from school, Christy played music as Jennifer and Dan sat quietly and listened. Between songs, Christy stopped the music and said, "I notice how both of you are quietly listening to the music and are not fighting. I want you to know that I am proud of you for getting along with each other." In this case, Jennifer and Dan were getting along. They weren't fighting or trying to annoy each other. Much to Christy's surprise, the more she deliberately reinforced Jennifer and Dan when they *weren't* fighting, the less they fought. From the behaviorist's point of view, there is nothing magical about human behavior — it is simply learned in reference to positive and negative consequences.

Encouraging Parental Consistency

Changing the behavior of children occurs most quickly when parents act together as a unit. In the case of John and Mary who identified the five values and behaviors, they cooperated in independently observing and reinforcing their children for the desired behaviors. Such cooperation is not always the case. Jose and Maria had three children but disagreed about what values were important (e.g. she thought having the children say the blessing at dinner was important while he thought it was a joke), what behaviors they wanted their children to develop (e.g. he wanted the children to say "yes, sir" and "yes, ma'am" while she thought a polite "yes" and "no" were appropriate), and what consequences to levy (e.g. he felt the belt was the way to go while she preferred withdrawing privileges). The result was a disaster. The children were confronted with two sets of values, expectations, and consequences with the result that they avoided the belt (did what their father said) but ignored their mother.

Parental consistency is imperative if children are to learn the desired behavior. In the absence of such consistency, the therapist should inform the parents that there will be no positive behavioral changes on the part of their children and that therapy will be a waste of time and money.

The problem of parents differing on what behaviors they want in their children also surfaces when the parents are remarried and bring children from previous relationships. The strategy most likely to result in behavior change in the child is to get the biological parent to take responsibility for monitoring and providing consequences and for the nonbiological parent to either be supportive or "not interfere." In effect, the nonbiological parent lets the biological parent do as he or she wishes. If the nonbiological parent cannot adopt this position, does not support the biological parent, and interferes with the strategies of the biological parent, the results will be catastrophic. The child's behavior will not change and the marital conflict will escalate to the boiling point. Under such conditions, the therapist might ask the parents to work on their marriage to resolve their conflict issues and later return to the issue of parenting consistency.

Encouraging Parental Patience

It is important that the therapist keep the expectations of the parents realistic in terms of how long it will take for their children to consistently engage in the desirable behavior. Just as fighting between siblings, yelling in the house, and tracking mud in the house did not become a pattern immediately, so it will take time for the children to experience the new consequences before they begin to change their behavior. A safe prediction (by the therapist) about how long it will take the parents to achieve their goal will be based on the parents' motivation and commitment, the frequency with which the behavior of the child occurs, and the frequency with which the parents are consistent in delivering consequences for the child's behavior. The therapist can tell the parents that if the behaviors of concern occur at a high frequency and if they will consistently "catch their children engaging in the behavior they want" and consistently provide negative consequences for behaviors they do not want, they can expect to see progress (decrease in negative behavior and increase in positive behavior) at the end of the third week (or sooner). Of course, the therapist will ask the parents to keep thorough records of what behaviors are occurring, when, and with what consequences. While new behaviors will take time to become a part of the child's behavioral repertoire, changes will occur sooner rather than later if the parents will provide the appropriate consequences.

A Treatment Program for Disruptive School Behavior

As noted earlier, assessment includes identifying what antecedents are associated with the problem behavior. Keyshaun is in the third grade and extremely bright. He excels in math and reading. However, he disrupts (talks, walks around) the classroom frequently, which results in his teacher sending him to the office, where the principal calls his mother. Both his teacher and principal are frustrated and have tried numerous strategies to get Keyshaun to stop misbehaving. Some of the interventions have included Keyshaun being required to sit alone at lunch, being suspended "in school," calling his parents, and being suspended out of school.

Keyshaun's mother was asked by the principal to have him evaluated for medication and have him involved in therapy. The therapist recommended assessing Keyshaun's behavior in the school setting to find out what the antecedents and consequences for his misbehavior were.

Data Provided by Mother

Below is the ABC reporting form. Recall that A = antecedents, B = behavior, and C = consequences. The ABC reporting form provided Keyshaun's mother and the data she provided follow:

Date: 5-20-08   Time of Day: 12:40 PM

1. What behavior did the child engage in that was a problem?

    __ fighting   __ running away   __ breaks things   __ tantrum

    X_ refusing to follow rules (describe: *Keyshaun refused to stay quiet when he finished his desk work.*)

    __ aggression (describe) _____

    X_ other: *Hits his desk with his hand*

2. What was the child doing just before the problematic behavior occurred?

    X school work (what? *Keyshaun had finished his math sheet; other students were still working.*)

    __ asked to do something (what?) _____

    __ asked not to do something (what?) _____

    __ told to stop doing something (what?) _____

3. What other people were in the room when the behavior occurred?

    __ mom   __ dad   __ sister   __ brother   X teacher   X classmates

    __ people in store   __ other _____

4. Where was the child when the behavior started?

    __ outside   X classroom   __ kitchen   __ bedroom   __ living room   __ in car   __ grocery store

    __ shopping   __ restaurant

    __ other (where?) _____

    __ other (where?) _____

5. What happened to the child immediately after the child engaged in the behavior?

    __ taken from the room   __ spanked   __ sat in time out   X spoken to by the teacher

    __ left alone   __ grounded

Mrs. Lanier, Keyshaun's teacher, collected data for several days so that his mother could give Keyshaun's therapist enough data to observe a pattern. The data revealed that when Keyshaun completed his work, he began to talk to other students or slapped his desk with his hand so as to make a noise/gain attention.

To begin to change the disruptive behavior, the therapist recommended that the teacher ask Keyshaun to engage in behavior incompatible with disruptive behavior (**antecedent strategy**) such as asking him to wipe the board or begin on his next assignment. The intervention plan follows:

Behavior Intervention Plan for Keyshaun

Name: Keyshaun

Reason for Intervention Plan: Classroom disruptions are unacceptable and interfere with the teacher's ability to teach/manage the classroom. Keyshaun's behavior has become disruptive and must stop.
Target Behaviors: "Disruptive Behavior" — Leaving desk without teacher's permission, speaking to others while class is engaged in seat-work and striking desk with a pencil or other object.
Frequency Reduction Goal: To reduce the frequency with which Keyshaun engaged in the target behaviors. His baseline frequency of disruptive behavior was once a day or five episodes per week. Over a three-week period, the goal was to drop the disruptive behavior to zero.

A theme of this book is that behavior that is being maintained is being reinforced. The therapist identified the reinforcers of Keyshaun's disruptive behavior as: 1. Attention from teacher, principal and peers. When Keyshaun was disruptive, his teacher would talk to him, take him to the principal's office and peers would look on in wonder. When Keyshaun was not disruptive, he was ignored. 2. Going to the principal's office was more reinforcing than sitting at his desk where he was bored, 3. Getting out of work was also a consequence of being disruptive since he would no longer be expected to sit at his desk and work if he were in the principal's office. 4. TV. If Keyshaun was lucky, his mother would come to school and take him home where he could watch TV or play video games. It comes as no surprise that being disruptive resulted in enormous payoffs for Keyshaun.

What alternative behaviors Keyshaun could engage in when he finished his math work:

Wipe the board

Read his library book

Draw

Color

Help the assistant collect papers when other students finish

Take attendance sheets to the office or other errands

Complete work from other subjects

Help other students

Keyshaun was asked to select three activities he would engage in when he finished his work. He chose to draw, take attendance sheets to the office and help other students. It is important to note that his helping of other students was carefully supervised by the teacher who made sure Keyshaun knew how to encourage the student being helped as well as how to be patient when the other student was having trouble. Keyshaun liked to have fun and joke around with other students, so his teacher was careful to keep an eye on him as he helped other students complete their work.

Reinforcers were agreed upon that Keyshaun could obtain when he engaged in any of the target behaviors when he finished his work. It is important to note that because his primary motivation to disrupt was to end boredom, the use of these strategies alone could have been useful for changing his behavior. However, there is the added issue of other reinforcers he would gain for his misbehavior, such as classroom attention and time spent with the principal in the principal's office.

To make clear what behaviors Keyshaun was expected to engage in, a behavior contract was developed as follows:

Keyshaun's Behavior Contract
2/20/08

When Keyshaun finishes his seat-work and draws, takes attendance sheets to the office for Mrs. Lanier, or helps other students with their desk work (without making noise or being disruptive), he may choose one of the following rewards. If he does not draw, etc., he forfeits the right to these rewards but will have the opportunity to try again the next day.

Rewards include:
1. Read from a book to the class after they have finished their work.
2. Visit the principal, Mr. Frank, to show him his completed work.
3. Go to the office to call his mother to tell her about his day.
4. Wipe the board or other chore suggested by the teacher.

Keyshaun _____   Mrs. Lanier _____

The behavior contract sets up Keyshaun for being successful at changing his disruptive behavior. He learns what behaviors to engage in that will earn him the relief from boredom he needs. The contract also rewards him for helping others. By intervening on the antecedent side of the behavioral sequence, Keyshaun's disruptive behaviors become less reinforcing. If Keyshaun does not engage in the target behaviors, he not only forfeits the rewards but will be separated from the rest of the class and not allowed to interact with teachers or students.

A Treatment Program for Disrespectful Behavior

Taylor is an energetic young lady who is six years old. Her parents described her as very intelligent and a natural born leader. She is an only child and has the benefit of much of her parents' attention. Her parents complained that she had become defiant and call them names such as "jerk" and "bitch." Although they explained to Taylor that she could not call them names, Taylor did so anyway.

Taylor's parents were asked to complete the ABC Form which provided information about what antecedents happened before and what consequences followed the behavior.

ABC Form for Taylor

Date: 2/10/08 Time of Day: 6:40 PM

1. What behavior did the child engage in that was problematic?

    __ fighting   __ running away   __ breaks things   __ tantrum

    __ refusing to follow rules (describe) _____

    __ aggression (describe) _____

    X_ other: *Called mother a "bitch."*

2. What was the child doing just before the problematic behavior occurred?

    __ school work (what?)_____

    X_ asked to do something (what?) *She was asked to begin taking her bath.*

    __ asked not to do something (what?) _____

    __ told to stop doing something (what?) _____

3. What other people were in the room when the behavior occurred?

    X_ mom   __ dad   __ sister   __ brother   __ teacher   ___ classmates

    __ people in store   __ other _____

4. Where was he/she when the behavior started?

__ outside   __ classroom   __ kitchen   __ bedroom   <u>X</u> living room   __ in car

__ grocery store   __ shopping   __ restaurant

__ other (where?) _____

__ other (where?) _____

5. What happened to the child immediately after the child engaged in the behavior?

__ taken from the room   __ spanked   __ sat in time out   <u>X</u> spoken to   __ left alone   __ grounded

Taylor's parents completed several ABC reports on different days and brought them to the next therapy session. The data revealed that the name calling was most frequent in the evening, primarily after dinner. An argument over what Taylor was to do after dinner (antecedent) always preceded the name calling.

Taylor's parents had tried punishing her by removing her CD player when she called them names. The effect was minimal in that after the CD was returned, Taylor would revert to name calling. The therapist noted that when Taylor argued with her parents and called them names, she ended up not taking a bath and was able to stay up and play longer before going to bed.

The therapist suggested an antecedent intervention whereby when Taylor displayed good manners (did not call her mother a "bitch") after dinner, she was allowed to take a shower. Taylor had never taken a shower before and she was intrigued with the idea. Taylor's contract:

Taylor's Shower Contract
3/17/08

When Taylor is polite to her parents and does not call her mother a bitch, she will earn the right to take a shower instead of a bath. If she is impolite and calls her mother a bitch, she will go to bed immediately and forfeit taking a shower. However, she will be able to try again the following night.

Taylor _____   Mom and Dad _____

Because Taylor was allowed to take a shower instead of a bath, stalling during her nightly routine stopped. The name calling and arguments also became less frequent and less intense.

Other Behavior Problems of Young Children

In addition to the disruptive school and verbal abuse behaviors presented above, parents of young children are sometimes concerned that their children will not eat their vegetables and will not do what they are asked to do.

Eating Vegetables

Parents struggle with getting children to eat nutritious food. Children often complain, cry, and refuse to eat when presented with only vegetables. Parents typically want to avoid the aversive behavior so give the child what he or she wants for food. Getting children to eat vegetables or whatever requires that parents arrange the consequences so that children eat them. "Eat your broccoli and then you can eat ice cream" is usually met with the child's protests so that the parent gives in. Doing so teaches the child "I can eat what I want as long as I pitch a fit about it."

If the parents' goal is for the child to eat certain foods, the child should be presented with the green beans and told to "try these and you can play video games after dinner and stay up an extra 15 minutes." If the child says "no," the parent should not force the issue, let the child eat the hot dog or whatever, but no video games after dinner and to bed at the regular time. The next night, the parent should try other consequences to find what works. In effect, a menu of reinforcers should be identified (e.g. having a friend sleep over on Friday night, watching a favorite video, swimming, etc.) and these used as consequences for the desirable behavior. The parent will find what works since the child will simply choose to engage in a mildly aversive behavior (e.g. green beans) in order to get a powerful positive (e.g. video game time). What the parent needs to avoid is giving a great deal of attention to the child who does not eat his or her green beans. When the child says, "No, I don't want those beans" the parent should say softly "OK" and not get caught up in a battle/argument which may become very reinforcing to the child since it is parental attention.

Compliance

Getting the child to do as asked is a major concern of both parents. From "clean your room" to "turn off the TV and come to dinner" to "put that candy down," parents want their children to do as asked. Compliance is no secret. Children comply with their parents' request when the positive consequences of doing so are greater than the negative consequences of not doing so. Shaping should be used to teach the child to comply. Recall that shaping is the reinforcing of small units of behavior toward the terminal goal. Getting the child to stop playing a video game and come to dinner is not easy. However, if the child has been reinforced for compliance in other contexts, the child is more likely to be compliant in regard to terminating video play.

Shaping compliance involves making requests of the child when it is easy for the child to comply and then reinforcing the child. For example, while sitting at the dinner table, the parent may ask the child to "pass the salt please." When the child does so, the parent should say, "Thank you for passing the salt; you did what I asked you to do. Let's go eat ice cream." These types of scenarios, where the child is asked to do something simple and then reinforced (at least verbally), help to build in the response pattern of the child to do as asked.

Getting the child to turn off the video game would involve sitting down with the child and saying, "One of our family rules is that you do what mommy and daddy ask you to do. For example, even though it is fun to play video games, when I ask you to stop, it is important that you do so if you want the video game left in the room for you to play with it. Let's practice. You play the video game and I will ask you to stop. If you stop, I will let you keep playing the game. If you do not stop, I will remove the video game from your room." Given these consequences, the child will stop playing the video game when asked.

Chapter 4

Case Histories: Young Children

Before I got married I had six theories about bringing up children;
now I have six children and no theories.

John Wilmot, Earl of Rochester (1647–1680)

The following case histories are behavioral interventions with young children (ages five to eleven). We present some successful, and as happens in any therapy, some unsuccessful cases. In the descriptions to follow, demographic information has been changed to protect the identity of the parents and their children.

Case 1: Smearing Feces

Claudia is a bright and spirited young lady of five years. Her parents, Jeff and Heather, are also very bright and ultra-successful in their careers. Heather, an up-and-coming vice president for a major corporation, is going back to school to complete an MBA. Jeff is the regional director for a major clothing chain and must spend several nights a month away from the family. Jeff and Heather were very anxious as they noted that they had recently been called during the day to their daughter's day care center because Claudia had wiped feces on the bathroom wall. Her teachers noted that this behavior had occurred on three occasions and that Claudia's behavior posed a health risk to the other children; if she did not stop, she would no longer be allowed at day care.

ABC reports completed by the teachers and parents revealed several patterns in regard to Claudia's feces-smearing behavior. It usually occurred in the late morning before lunch when teachers would allow Claudia to enter the bathroom and would not concern themselves with her again until she called the teachers into the bathroom for help. When the teachers did not come quickly, Claudia smeared feces on the bathroom walls. Once teachers discovered the mess, they were aghast, which Claudia experienced as attention. In addition, Claudia's parents were called and came to school to take her home for the remainder of the day. Hence, the "reward" from Claudia's perspective for smearing feces on the bathroom wall was attention from both teachers and parents and being driven home where she could watch TV.

The therapist recommended to the parents that they suggest to the day care teachers that they go with Claudia to the bathroom and praise her when she used the toilet, flushed it, and washed her hands. Such reinforcement seemed to reduce the frequency with which Claudia smeared feces. However, data revealed that when Claudia was denied a favorite item (e.g. more Kool Aid) or activity (e.g. play), she would go to the bathroom and smear feces.

The therapist suggested reinforcement for positive behavior. Claudia's parents agreed to call the school and, if she was having a good day (e.g. no feces smearing), they were to take the rest of the day off and pick Claudia up from school to have fun for the remainder of the day. If they called the school and Claudia had smeared feces, the parents were not to pick her up and instead, teachers would make Claudia clean up the mess and deny her the privilege of playing on the playground with the rest of the children at recess. Hence, the consequence for not smearing feces was time with parents; the consequence for smearing feces was no parents, clean up the mess herself, and no playing on the playground with other children.

Over time, Claudia's smearing of feces reduced to zero. To ensure that the desirable behavior continued, the parents would randomly call the school and come to pick up Claudia on a "good day." However, after six months, the parents no longer needed to go to school as Claudia was getting attention at school from her teachers and she was enjoying playing with her friends of the playground.

Case 2: Sleeping in Parents' Bed

Edna is a bright ten-year-old who is doing well at school and makes excellent grades. She has friends, enjoys riding her bike, and plays make-believe with them. She also sleeps in her parents' bed. Darryl and Joyce would like for Edna to sleep in her own bed. When the parents came to therapy, Edna slept in the bed with Darryl while Joyce slept on the couch. Not only was Edna not learning to sleep independently in her own bed, Darryl and Joyce were not sleeping together — something both were angry and resentful about.

The intervention involved several steps. The first was to assess how many nights per week Edna slept in the same bed with her father. ABC forms were not needed since her parents described this pattern occurred every night. Edna had not slept in her own room for years — neither parent could remember the last time she slept in her own room. The explanation for this bizarre behavior was that Edna was afraid that "something was in her closet," which made her uncomfortable sleeping alone in her room (the new behavioral goal).

Because Edna's parents worried about her emotional state, they agreed that Edna would sleep on the floor beside their marital bed. They made a small, comfortable area for Edna to sleep on and contracted with her that if she slept on the floor, she would earn the privilege to eat pancakes (her favorite food) the following morning.

Reports from the parents revealed that Edna was able to sleep beside their bed overnight on six of seven nights. Consistent with the principle of shaping, the second week, Edna's sleeping area was moved to the foot of the marital bed where she slept for three weeks. Edna continued to earn pancakes and other privileges, such as extra time with her friends and the privilege to have extra computer time the morning/days she slept at the foot of the marital bed.

As Edna's "bed" was slowly being moved further away from the marital bed, one evening at the regular appointment, Edna's mother proudly declared that her daughter had slept in her own bed every night for the past week. Joyce went on to describe that she had been at a sale of bed linens and had bought sheets with a high thread count. Edna had stretched out on the sheets, which felt to her like silk, and told her mother that she would like to sleep on these new sheets.

This example illustrates a case where antecedent interventions (sleeping on new, more comfortable sheets) as well as shaping (gradual removal of the child from the parents' bed) worked together to change the behavior. It is also important to note that having Edna sleep on new sheets was not the therapist's idea. Sometimes therapists learn the best strategies from their clients!

Case 3: Staying Up until 3:00 AM

Trevor is a three-year-old boy who lives with his mother and grandmother. His mother says that Trevor is difficult to parent, as he ignores his mother's and grandmother's directions, throws tantrum,s and generally engages in disrespectful behavior with his mother and grandmother. His mother also reported that Trevor stays up until 2:00 or 3:00 AM. Although there were many behaviors the therapist could have focused on, having Trevor go to bed earlier, at 8:00 PM, became the goal.

Trevor's grandmother and mother were asked to keep records of his sleeping behavior. The data revealed that Trevor was staying up until two or three o'clock in the morning before going to sleep. When asked about bedtime routines, Trevor's mother noted that she tried to put Trevor to bed at ten o'clock but he would cry and leave the room. She also described the home as loud as family often dropped by to visit later in the evening, the volume of the television was usually high, or family members would sometimes speak loudly to one another.

The therapist also asked Trevor's mother to keep records of his sleeping during the day. Data revealed that Trevor slept three to four hours each day during the day. The first goal of therapy was to reduce the amount of time Trevor slept during the day — Trevor's mother was instructed to allow him to have two naps — one in the morning and one in the afternoon for a maximum of thirty minutes. By restricting Trevor's sleep during the day, he would be ready to sleep at night.

The therapist recommended a new bedtime routine whereby Trevor's mom would turn off the television at 7:00, give him his bath, and dress him in his pajamas so that he was in the bed by 7:30. From then until 8:00 PM his mom would read to him. He would then say his prayers, she would kiss him good night, and leave the room. If he got up and cried, she would gently hold his shoulders and direct him back to bed. If he was still crying, she would simply stay with him until he stopped crying.

The therapist also emphasized the importance of the mother getting control of her household so that the television was played at a low volume and adults were asked to speak softly (or go outside). Trevor was resistant to the new schedule for the first few nights so his afternoon nap was eliminated. The result was that Trevor, while irritable, was more tired and more vulnerable to going to sleep at 8:30. Both Trevor's mother and grandmother noted that by changing his schedule, his tantrums, although not eliminated, became less frequent and less of an issue.

Case 4: Cursing Parents

When Samantha was two, she would often look at her parents and with a stern look on her face and a pointed finger, say, "No". Her parents, Mike and Jackie, thought this behavior was most amusing. As Samantha grew, her protests and acts of defiance became more annoying to her parents. Her parents became concerned, purchased a book on dealing with difficult children, and tried some of the strategies. When Samantha's behavior did not improve, they abandoned the program and started giving in to Samantha's tantrums.

Samantha also became impossible to control in social situations. One evening when her parents took her with them to the house of one of their friends, Samantha was inconsolable when told that the hostess's food was all that was available, spilled her drink on the carpet, and pulled items out of the drawers in the bedroom. When asked to sit at the table with the rest of the children, Samantha turned the other way and shouted, "BITCH." The parents scheduled a therapy appointment the following Monday.

Jackie and Mike were asked to keep ABC records on Samantha's behaviors which upset them. A typical ABC report looked like the following:

Date: 5-12-08   Time of Day: 5:58 PM

1. What behavior did you see?

   __ fighting   __ running away   __ breaks things   __ tantrum

   X_ refusing to follow rules (describe: *Samantha said, "bitch" to her mother*)

___ aggression (describe) _____

___ other _____

2. What happened before Samantha engaging in the undesirable behavior?

___ school work (what?) _____

___ asked to do something (what?) _____

___ asked not to do something (what?) _____

X_ told to stop doing something (what? *She was arguing with her parents.*)

3. Who was around when Samantha engaged in the inappropriate behavior started?

X_ mom X_ dad   ___ sister   ___ brother   ___ teacher   ___ classmates

___ people in store   ___ other _____

4. Where was Samantha when the behavior started?

___ outside   ___ classroom   ___ kitchen   ___ bedroom   X_ living room   ___ in car

___ grocery store   ___ shopping   ___ restaurant

___ other (where?) _____

___ other (where?) _____

5. What did the parents do when Samantha engaged in the inappropriate behavior?

___ taken from the room   ___ spanked   ___ sat in time out   X_ spoken to   ___ left alone   ___ grounded

As the data showed, cursing was preceded by being involved in an argument with her parents. The argument most often started when the parents asked Samantha to do something and she refused. The interaction escalated with the parents getting angry and Samantha being frustrated since she did not get her way. At this time, Samantha blurted out "bitch" or "loser" or "asshole".

The therapist suggested that the parents talk softly to Samantha so as not to allow an argument to develop, to ignore/walk away when cursing behavior occurred, and to only allow Samantha to do things she enjoyed when she engaged in appropriate behavior.

As Samantha's parents became consistent in their new behavior toward Samantha, she learned that there was no payoff for or cursing with her parents — they simply ignored her. In addition, they withdrew privileges (no television or phone) when she cursed. Subsequent records revealed that Samantha's cursing dropped to zero.

Case 5: Disrespecting Nonbiological Parent's Requests

Remus and Jessica are a remarried couple each with a pre-teen from a previous marriage, Tonya and Andrew. Each parent complained that their nonbiological child talked back, yelled, and did not do as requested. Only the biological parent could control his or her own biological child. The result was frustration on the part of each parent for having a child be impolite to them. The couple also reported stress in their marriage over the respective disrespectful children.

ABC reports revealed a number of behavioral problems — fighting between the stepsiblings, fighting between the parents and the respective nonbiological children, and noncompliance over study behavior, completing chores, and going to bed on time. In consultation with the therapist, new house rules were established.

1. Inside "quiet" voices inside the house, outside "loud" voices outside the house

2. Keep hands and feet to yourself

3. Say "please" and "thank you" when speaking to others

4. Do what both (including nonbiological) parents say

Potential rewards for engaging in each of the above behaviors were identified as follows:

1. Draw a present from the surprise box

2. Have a friend over to spend the night

3. Ice cream after supper

4. Watch television

5. Stay up an extra fifteen minutes each night with parents

The parents were to also make clear that there would be negative consequences for noncompliance, including:

1. No friends could visit the house or stay overnight

2. No telephone calls to friends

3. No television or computer games for twenty-four hours

4. No visiting with friends at their home

The parents agreed to follow the same house rules in terms of being polite, inside voices, etc. In effect, they would serve as models for the appropriate behavior.

Parents also noted that they would look for times when their children were engaging in the appropriate behavior, to catch their children being good. Both parents reported that the behavior of the children changed in the desired direction — the children talked back less, said "please" and "thank you" more often. The children also began to study more and go to bed on time. These behaviors changed only after the parents withheld all privileges such as phone, TV, and friends. Once the children discovered that access to these reinforcers was through the behavior identified by their parents, they changed their behavior to get the reward and avoid the negative consequences. However, the parents noted that the kids tested them the first week to find out that they (the parents) were going to follow through with the consequences. The parents held fast and the behavior of the children changed.

The issue of the nonbiological child being disrespectful to the nonbiological parent disappeared when each parent told their respective biological child that their respective privileges and punishments were contingent on doing what the nonbiological parent said. Once the children learned they could not "get away with bullying the nonbiological parent," they stopped. Consistency was the key to the success of this family getting a grip on their pre-teens.

Case 6: Getting Child to Help Sick Mother

Devon is eight years old and is doing well at school. His mother, Linda, has been diagnosed with a degenerative disease that affects her central nervous system. She needs her son to help her with chores and she does not have the energy to fight with him. Indeed, Linda noted that she has days where she can't get around and needs help in the house. She noted that although Devon was not disagreeable or disrespectful towards her, she would like to have more help around the house, particularly on days she wasn't feeling well. She reported that she had to remind Devon to clean his room and she nagged him to pick up after himself when he left toys and clothes strewn throughout the house. She also had drifted into doing the chores herself since she did not have the energy to nag him into doing them.

Devon's mother agreed to monitor his activities at home and reward him for chore completion. She was not to remind him when a chore was not done. Chores would be posted on the refrigerator for his reference. Because Linda was committed to these stipulations, it was agreed that the therapist would help her devise a token system to reward his chore completion behaviors.

Linda identified the things that motivated Devon — ice cream, eat at a pizza restaurant, play video games, watch television and play outside with his friends. A token system was devised whereby Devon could earn tokens by doing what his mom wanted and then trade these in for what he wanted. For example, taking the trash out was worth one token, vacuuming the den floor was worth one token, and vacuuming his room was worth one token.

Below is the list of reinforcers and the number of tokens Devon must earn to get them:

Ice cream: six tokens

Eating at favored restaurant: six tokens

Playing video game for thirty minutes: two tokens

Watching television for thirty minutes: two tokens

Fifteen extra minutes outside: one token

Inviting a friend over to play for an hour: one token

Linda also agreed to pay particular attention to the times when he did something helpful that she did not ask him to do. For example, when Devon did a chore or task without having to be told, he was to be given a token. She continued not reminding him to do his chores.

Linda also agreed to hug, kiss, and praise Devon when he received a token. She was to give him the token and praise him at the same time. At the next session, Linda reported an enormous difference in Devon's behavior. She noted that he had been very helpful around the house and had begun looking for things to do to earn more tokens.

Case 7: Failing to Provide Records — Parental Noncompliance

In behavioral family therapy, parents become the main agents of change as they become instrumental in the administration of positive and negative consequences to effect new behavior in their children. Behavioral family therapy will only be effective to the degree that parents carry out the recommendations of the therapist.

One example of an unsuccessful behavioral intervention is the case of Nicolas who was referred by his pediatrician. When his mother brought Nicolas to therapy, he was withdrawn, looked down, and did not respond to the questions designed to invite discussion. The behavioral goal of the mother for her child was "not being depressed." Behaviors incompatible with depression were defined as "looking one in the eye when talking," "responding to questions," "initiating interaction/talk," "playing with friends," and "playing with sister." ABC sheets were given to the mother who was asked to keep a record of Nicolas' "being happy/energetic behavior."

The mother returned to therapy but did not bring the ABC sheets. She reported that Nicolas was still sad but provided no data regarding the alternative behaviors. The therapist discussed the importance of record keeping and the mother agreed to keep the records and return the following week. The mother canceled the next appointment.

Case 8: Traveling to Grandma's in the Family Van

Shamika and Regionald are parents of Nicki and Augusta. The parents came to therapy concerned that they had an upcoming eleven-hour trip to see their children's grandmother and feared that the children's bickering would make the trip intolerable. Baseline data revealed that Nicki and Augusta, ages six and nine, routinely fought with each other whenever they were in the back seat of the family van. Their fighting had escalated to the point that, on one occasion, Shamika had to stop the van. She had "lost it" and yelled at the kids, who ended up crying. Clearly the bickering children in the back seat made traveling in the van unsafe.

The therapist identified the desirable behaviors of the children as "staying in one's seat without touching the other sibling" and "talking softly to one's sibling." Since the trip to grandma's was two weeks away, the therapist recommended some "practice trips" whereby the children would be reinforced for the desirable behaviors.

The parents were to tell their children:

> It is important that we are safe when traveling in the van and important that when you are in the van that you stay in your car seat, keep your hands to yourself, and talk softly to your sibling. For doing so, mommy and daddy will give you tokens which you can trade in for things you want like playing handheld video games and using your earphones. In addition, tokens can also be exchanged for driving to get ice cream or a soft drink. If you get out of your seat, touch your sibling, or speak loudly (yell) to your sibling, you will earn no tokens and lose the privilege to play your video game and listen to your music. And, we will not stop for ice cream or a soft drink.

Using the principle of shaping, rewarding small units of behavior toward the terminal goal, the parents were asked to take three practice trips a week leading up to the big eleven-hour grandmother trip. During the first practice trip, the parents were to tell the children that they were going to take a short drive so that they could find out how easy it was to earn tokens for being safe in the car. The father was to drive one block and the mother was to turn around and give each child a token for "sitting in your seat, not touching each other, and not talking or talking softly with each other." After another three blocks, the mother was to repeat the same behavior of noticing that the children were engaging in the desired behavior and give them another token. The father was then to drive another five blocks and to end up at a place like McDonald's where the children could get ice cream or a soft drink. In effect, the children would learn that sitting in their own seat, not touching each other, and talking softly resulted in good things for them. The parents were to have a total of six "practice drives" before the "grandmother trip."

When the day of the trip arrived, the children were anxious to sit in their seats, keep their hands to themselves, and speak softly to each other. The mother would dispense tokens throughout the trip that the children could exchange for their video games and music/earphones. In addition, the children were told that when they stopped for lunch that they could get ice cream or a soft drink. The parents called the therapist on their return from grandma's and noted that while there was one fight that broke out between the kids the last hour of the return trip, for the most part, the trip was wonderful. The therapist noted that it was they, the parents, who were wonderful for taking the time to practice with their children before the trip so that when the grandma trip rolled around their children were accustomed to being safe (e.g. sitting in their car seat, not touching each other, etc.).

Case 9: Taking a Shower

Amy is eight years old and does not like to take a bath/shower. Sheila, her mother, noted that Amy argued with her about taking a bath to the point that Sheila would let her go for several days without one. But her mother feared that Amy's friends would eventually notice and may ostracize her because of her body odor.

The therapist suggested a behavior contract whereby Amy would agree to take a bath or shower four times a week in exchange for a vanilla milkshake at McDonald's. If she did not bathe four times a week, she would not earn a milkshake, but would have the opportunity to make another agreement next week.

In the first week, Amy bathed three times. Since doing so was definite progress, the therapist agreed that the following week if she bathed three times, she could earn a vanilla milkshake. In reality, the following week Amy bathed four times, the next week five, and the next week six. In effect, while Amy earned her vanilla milkshake each time, she found bathing reinforcing and began to do so since she enjoyed feeling clean. What started out as not bathing since this behavior was reinforced by the mother's attention/arguing changed to bathing due to reinforcement via a milkshake and finally reinforcement from verbal praise and the feeling of being clean.

Case 10: Stealing

Max is the only child of two parents going through a divorce. His mother recently moved in with her boyfriend. Max lived with his mother and visited his father on the weekend. Recently, Max's mother received a note from Max's teacher saying that Max has been caught stealing another student's personal property (book bag). The mother also noted that Max had stolen her boyfriend's wallet and his grandfather's money. On each occasion, Max denied stealing the items but eventually admitted the theft.

ABC reports revealed that Max's stealing behavior was being reinforced by attention from his mother, his father, and his grandfather. Each adult would spend a great deal of focused time with Max lecturing to him on the merits of honesty. Stealing is the one behavior Max could count on to get adult attention.

The therapist recommended reinforcing Max for not stealing. Max's mother noted that one of the things Max most enjoyed was to go to Baskin-Robbins for ice-cream and to play video games. The therapist asked the mother to tell Max that when she picked up Max each afternoon at school that she was going to search his book bag and that if there were no stolen items, she was to take him to Baskin-Robbins for ice cream and allow him to play video games when he got home. If there were stolen items in his book bag, they would go straight home and he would have no access to his video games and go to bed early.

Max's stealing behavior at school dropped to zero but he continued to steal at home from his mother's boyfriend. In effect, Max was being reinforced for honesty in one context but not in another. The therapist recommended a similar intervention in the home. Each day Max did not steal any money from her boyfriend, he was allowed to watch television and stay up an extra fifteen minutes. If he was found stealing, his television privileges were cut off and he was to go to bed fifteen minutes earlier. While the therapist assumed that the home intervention strategy worked, the mother canceled the follow-up appointment.

Case 11: Hitting Sibling

A couple complained that their five-year-old daughter Tabitha had the habit of hitting her two-year-old brother. ABC reports revealed that this occurred about twice a week. The "hits" were not hard but aggressive pushes. The therapist recommended never leaving Tabitha alone with the two-year-old and regularly praising Tabitha when she was in the presence of her brother. Phrases such as "you are such a wonderful sister playing so gently with your brother," "you are so kind to your baby brother," and "he loves for you to rub his arms gently" were designed to reinforce Tabitha for playing softly with the-two-year-old. The parents were also to take Tabitha to McDonald's on the weekend as they reminded her what a gentle-playing sister she was. The hitting behaviors dropped to zero on subsequent recordings.

Chapter 5

Adolescents: Problems and Solutions

If you aren't doing behavior contracts with adolescents, you aren't doing therapy.

Louise Sammons

A parent of two young children complained to her neighbor that her kids were driving her crazy. "It gets worse," replied the parent of three teenagers. Indeed, research on parental satisfaction across the family life cycle reveals that the teen years are the most difficult. "When the kids are between the ages of thirteen and eighteen, it's the bottom," lamented one dad. In this chapter, we identify the reasons adolescence is such a challenge for parents, review the typical problems parents face with their teenagers, and specify the behavior family therapist's intervention strategies to help parents get through these most difficult years.

Why Adolescence Is a Difficult Period

Three reasons account for adolescence being a difficult period for parents: independence, money, and serious errors in judgment.

Struggle for Independence

Families are systems which involve the upward mobility of children (over time the roles reverse as parents end up being dependent on their children). Teenagers are no longer completely dependent on their parents. Nor are they capable of being completely independent of them. So while teenagers may resent the structure parents necessarily impose on them (when they are expected to be in from a date and the amount of time they are expected to study), they are dependent on their parents for food, shelter, transportation, etc.

Adolescents, who test the outer limits of what his or her parents will tolerate, confirm that the parents are on schedule with their parenting. A child who thinks for himself/herself and asks questions reflects the qualities of independence that parents should be proud of. To have a child who accepts everything without question is a drone no parent can be proud of — a child who will have difficulty surviving in the adult world just ahead. But while parents may silently be proud of their son's or daughter's emerging independence, channeling and containing their independence is yet another matter.

Expensive for the Family Budget

Parents note that adolescents are more expensive than when they were younger. From food (they eat more), to transportation, to various activities (including a car), to clothes (sometimes only name brands will do), it all costs money — lots of it. U.S. Census figures published for 2008 for these respective costs per child on an annual basis for a middle-income family were $2,380, $2180, and $730. And near the end of adolescence, parents learn of application fees for college, first semester tuition, dorm room expenses — it never ends.

Hence, adolescence is a difficult time for parents. Not only do they need to hold the reins tight so that the adolescent does not career off the main road into a ditch (drug abuse, unplanned pregnancy), they need to keep a check on their spending habits. However, adolescence is also a time of joy. Parents can relish in the fact that their offspring are becoming young adults, learning about life, and enjoying themselves.

Tragic Adolescent Decisions

Adolescence is also a scary time for parents who fear their children will exercise poor judgment — get drunk, abuse drugs, contract a sexually transmitted disease, or have an unplanned pregnancy. These fears are not unfounded. The second author is friends with parents whose son got drunk one night and poured gasoline on a couch outside his girlfriend's apartment as a prank. The fire raged out of control and four friends died in the fire. The son, age eighteen, was sentenced to life in prison without the possibility of parole — a parent's worst nightmare.

Drug abuse is another concern. The second author also knows of parents whose son sneaked out of the house at night to spend the night with a peer. The agenda was to get high and have a wild night. They did. The son did not wake up the next morning and was in a coma. It is now three years later. The son is brain damaged from the drug cocktail he took that one night and will be in a bed until death. He was seventeen at the time of the overdose.

Sexual behavior is another fear of parents. A mix of alcohol and drugs alters the judgment of teens so that having sex without a condom becomes easy. The result is a sexually transmitted infection that affects the child's self esteem, relationships with others, and fertility. HPV, genital warts, is the most frequent STI teens contract today (about 25 percent will do so before age eighteen).

Not only may the teen contract an STI (including herpes and HIV), but a pregnancy can result. The options of being a parent at age seventeen or having an abortion are decisions no seventeen-year-old or his/her parents want to deal with. Sarah Palin's family is an exception.

Creating the Right Context with Adolescents

A "snare" is an event that can wreck a teen's life from which he or she may never recover. Teens are vulnerable to the snares identified above in reference to alcohol/drug abuse, STIs, and teen pregnancy. One wrong decision and the teen's (and parents') lives are changed forever. To reduce the chances of one's teenager making bad choices, the parents must create an engaging context so that they stay "connected" to their son or daughter. Adolescents who get into trouble have career-focused parents who spend little time with their children and who expect them to grow up by themselves. It rarely happens. Rather, teens who flourish have parents who spend time with them and teachers who monitor their progress. The conditions under which teens seem to "stay out of trouble" and who "stay on track" include a family context of open communication (which involves discussing sex and drugs), orchestrating fun/family times with adolescents, monitoring teen activities, making clear rules, and following through with consequences. We now discuss each of these.

Keeping Communication Open (Stay in the Teen's World)

Teenagers sometimes shut out their parents since they view them as "out of it." The parents don't know who the winner of *American Idol* is, what the latest video game is, or the new DVD releases. The antidote is for the parents to learn about their teens' world — watch *American Idol*, pick up the controls of Grand Theft Auto, and look in the movie section of *USA Today* to learn "what's showing." Teens are not capable of getting into the parents' world, so parents must bridge the gap. The second author needed to "connect" with his two children, so he took scuba diving lessons with them. The three of them went on over 100 dives together.

Shared activities create the context for open communication between parents and their teens — talking about whatever, learning about their interests and thoughts. The goal is to establish the norm that talking occurs between parents and their teens so that the teens feel that the channel is open. Where parents and teens never spend time together, the teen feels his or her parents are not available to talk.

Discussing Sex and Drugs

Talking about sex and drugs should be part of the communication between parents and their teens. Research shows that children **are** influenced by their parents' values. A good place to start with teens is to give them an age-appropriate book which provides the nuts and bolts of sexuality. A specific book for girls is *Our Bodies, Ourselves: A New Edition for a New Era* by the Boston Women's Health Book Collective, Judy Norsigian, author (Touchtone, 2005). A similar book for boys is *My Body, My Self for Boys, Revised Third Edition (What's Happening to My Body?)* by Lynda Madaras and Area Madaras. Both books can be purchased through Amazon.com. One strategy for parents is to give the daughter or son the respective book, tell them that they want them to read the book and that the parent will ask them about the content.

Specific books for parents to help them talk with their teens about sex include: *The Real Truth About Teens and Sex: From Hooking Up to Friends with Benefits — What Teens Are Thinking, Doing, and Talking About, and How to Help Them Make Smart Choices* by Sabrina Weill (Berkley Publishers, 2005) and *Ten Talks Parents Must Have with Their Children About Sex and Character* by Pepper Schwartz and Dominic Cappello (Hyperion, 2000). These books are also available through Amazon.com.

The important point for parents is to make learning about sex OK and to make it OK for teens to read about it and OK to talk about it. Watching a movie together (e.g. *Juno* and *Knocked Up*) with teens is a great opportunity to slide into conversations about sexuality. A "don't have sex until you are married" will sometimes work if the parents and teens are evangelical Christians and attend worship services regularly. Parents who are more liberal might emphasize the value of waiting 'til one is older and involved/in love with the person to have intercourse — this is the message from teens who have already had intercourse. Use of a condom and being on birth control are musts. Parents should make both available to their teens. Over half of today's teens will have intercourse before they graduate from high school.

Websites also provide a great deal of information about sex. Parents should be made aware of "Go Ask Alice" http://www.goaskalice.columbia.edu/ and "Scarleteen" http://www.scarleteen.com/ and may want to pass these on to their teens.

Drug use should also be addressed. According to the U.S. Census Bureau in 2008, 27 percent of teens between the ages of twelve and seventeen admit to ever having used an illicit drug. The drug most teens have tried is marijuana (17 percent). In regard to alcohol use, 41 percent of teens between the ages of twelve and seventeen report having experienced alcohol (26 percent have smoked cigarettes). Parents should emphasize that drug use is against the law and something they should decide about later — for now, it is off the table. A too-loose "OK, if you don't get too much in you" can prove fatal if the teen gets in a car and drives.

Having Fun Times with Adolescents (So Parents Aren't Just the Police)

One way to enhance the influence parents have over their children is to do fun things with them. The pattern of going out to eat, seeing movies together, and taking family vacations should be established early and the therapist should encourage such family activities. As peers become more important to older teens, the interest of teens in family vacations will decrease. The family vacation with the teens should still occur; perhaps let them select where they would like to go.

Monitoring Teen Behavior
(Parents Need to Know Where Their Children Are, etc.)

A major source of "problems with teenagers" results from the parents taking their eye off the ball. Teenagers need constant monitoring. In a study by the second author, over 90 percent of college students admitted that they had lied to their parents about whom they were with and what they were doing. While the teen may have told mom "we're going shopping at the mall," in reality they were taking a joy ride smoking dope with a guy they had met at the beach. Bottom line — parents need to know where their children are, whom they are with, and what they are doing. While teens can still be deceptive, they (the teens) should know that their parents care about their well being and want to ensure that they are where they say they will be.

In response to the teen who says "you don't trust me," the answer is. . . . "I'm the parent and it is my role to make sure you are safe." If the teen has lied (and been caught) in the past, the parent may say, "I am simply giving you a chance to regain my trust by ensuring that you are where you say you will be."

Making Rules Clear

Teens flourish with structure. If they have no study time, no bedtime, no curfew, and no parameters for anything, they will flounder — studying won't happen and they are vulnerable to getting into trouble if they are allowed to stay out all night. Just as young children need "house" rules, teens need rules as they move into adulthood. However, rules are not enough. Consistency in consequating behavior is the key. Teens must learn that "when I follow the rules, good things happen; when I don't, bad things happen." One teen came home drunk to discover that use of his cell phone, car, and computer were ended for six months. Coming home drunk did not recur.

Following Through with Consequences

Nothing changes behavior but consequences. The teen who is asked to be home by midnight and who shows up at 1:00 AM with no consequences (since the parents are asleep) will stay out 'til 1:00 AM or later the next night. The teen who shows up at 1:00 AM to a parent waiting at the door who calmly takes the keys and says "you are grounded for a month" will certainly be on time in the future.

Parents are sometimes reluctant to consequate the negative behavior of their children. Parents fear their son or daughter will distance themselves by their own disapproval and shut the parent off. In effect, the teen is using consequences (withdrawal of approval/no talking) to teach the parent to be slack. When the parent looks the other way at a negative behavior (being late), the teen smiles, jokes, says "ah mom. . . . I just lost track of time. . . . wanna go shopping?" Reinforced for this behavior, the parent says "don't be late again" only to discover the teen is late again. And why not? There was no consequence for being late except parental disapproval which was not sufficient to deter the undesirable behavior.

The problem with teaching a teen that there are no consequences for negative behavior is that the teen learns a tragic lesson: "I can do as I want since nothing bad happens." They take this learning pattern to college where they skip class, drink nightly, and cheat on their partners. And why not? They assume "the teachers won't flunk me, nobody gets hurt if I drink, and my partner will forgive me."

The role of the parent is to teach the teen to survive in the adult world. Teaching these survival skills is hard work. Children will not like their parents if they are strict. Indeed, teens will punish their parents back. Only later, when teens go to college, get married, and have children of their own will they appreciate the value of structure and discipline. And, even then, they may not. No matter. What is important is that parents have taught their children to be responsible citizens who get up and go to work on time, etc. One dad told his teen, "I am here to be your parent, not your friend." Therapists play a role in socializing youth for society by making clear to parents how behavior is learned and how children can benefit from consistent consequences.

As noted earlier, just as negative consequences may be necessary to bring behavior under control (e.g. withdrawal of privileges for inappropriate behavior), reinforcing teens for positive behavior is just as important. Praise for one's teen engaging in study behavior, for being on time, for being polite, and for helping around the house is crucial to maintain those behaviors. The teen's self concept is also at stake. By making good grades, the teen can feel proud of himself/herself. When the teen is on time and polite, other people notice, appreciate, and may comment on. Everyone wins when the parents praise their children for positive behavior.

Problems Parents Have with Their Adolescents

Therapy with adolescents is very different than that with children. Adolescents have beliefs and a world view that work against them. One mother said of her teen, "he thinks he's bulletproof." This belief can have tragic catastrophic consequences since the teen can have a couple of beers, get behind the wheel, and have a fatal car wreck (killing not only himself or herself but others in the car).

Another view of the adolescent is "no one is telling me what to do." So when dad says lights out at 11:00 and AJ is up 'til 1:30 AM playing video games, the consequences are delayed: falling asleep in school, bad grades, being held back a grade. Parents must insist that their teens follow the rules. In this section we review some common problems parents have with their teenagers.

Arguing

Marcia, age fifteen, has jet black hair (dyed) and is fond of wearing black clothes like many of her friends. Rose, her mother, has been frustrated by the fights she has been having with Marcia. Rose came to therapy for relief of her stress with Marcia. Marcia's behavior was described as cursing, throwing things, slamming doors, etc. Rose explained their fighting as "we are both female."

Rose was asked to complete ABC reports for her daughter's various inappropriate behaviors and provided the following report.

Date: 3/17/09   Time of Day: 4:30 PM

1. What behaviors did you see?

__ fighting   __ running away   __ breaks things   __ tantrum

X refusing to follow rules (describe: *Marcia talked back and argued.*)

__ aggression (describe) _____

__ other_____

2. What was going on when the behavior occurred?

X school work (what? *Marcia was working on her homework.*)

__ asked to do something (what?) _____

__ asked not to do something (what?) _____

__ told to stop doing something (what?) _____

3. Who was in the house when the argument happened?

   X mom   __ dad   X sister   __ brother   __ teacher   __ classmates

   __ people in store   __ other _____

4. Where was Rose when the behavior started?

   __ outside   __ classroom   X kitchen   __ bedroom   __ living room   __ in car

   __ grocery store   __ shopping   __ restaurant

   __ other (where?) _____

   __ other (where?) _____

5. What happened after Marcia engaged in the inappropriate behavior?

   __ taken from the room   __ spanked   __ sat in time out   X spoken to   __ left alone   __ grounded

Rose returned the completed ABC reports to each session. After three weeks, Rose and the therapist noticed a pattern — the arguments began in the afternoon when Marcia was in her room doing homework and called to her mother in the kitchen for help. Soon the two women were fighting with each other. The antecedent condition for fighting was when Marcia called Rose for help with homework and the consequences were two reinforcers: 1. Rose gave Marcia her undivided attention and 2. Marcia got a break from doing homework when she was interacting with her mom. In fact, the longer the fight with her mom, the longer Marcia escaped working on her homework.

Another antecedent for the argument between Marcia and her mother was Rose's fatigue. Rose was a ninth grade music teacher at a local school and noted that she was exhausted when she got home in the afternoon. Such exhaustion resulted in her being vulnerable to fighting with Marcia. Hence, Rose's behavior as well as Marcia's was a target for intervention.

The intervention included Rose's helping Marcia with the first three math problems. When it became clear to Rose that Marcia could complete additional problems on her own, Rose was to leave the room while Marcia was to complete three additional problems on her own. When these three were completed, Marcia was to call her mother into the room to check the problems. If, for some reason, Marcia had difficulty completing the three problems on her own, she was to do as much as she could. After Marcia either completed the three problems on her own, or did as much as much she could, she was to tell her mom who would acknowledge her independent work: "I appreciate your trying to finish those problems on your own." Rose would then help Marcia complete the fourth problem and ask Marcia to complete the next three independently.

Rose returned to the following appointment reporting that the fights had stopped and Marcia was now completing her homework. Rose was instructed to increase the number of unassisted problems to five and to acknowledge Marcia's working independently. Rose was also to help Marcia with the sixth problem. In effect, the antecedent of Marcia's initiating an argument was changed from her working on homework alone to her working on homework with her mom. And, rather than be yelled at for interrupting Rose in the kitchen, Rose approached Marcia and thanked her for her independent work. Meanwhile, Rose found sitting down with Marcia and working homework with her much easier than being interrupted by Marcia in the kitchen. While Rose reported that another fight did break out, she noted the intensity was weaker and that the frequency of the arguments radically decreased. The last stage of the intervention was a gradual fading whereby Rose helped

Marcia less and less and Marcia worked on her homework independently more and more. Finally, Marcia finished all of her homework by herself which was followed by her mom acknowledging and praising her for working independently.

A comment about Rose's fatigue. It was clear to Rose that her fatigue at the end of the day contributed to her impatience with Marcia interrupting her during her homework. The therapist instructed Rose to take a deep breath before entering the area where Marcia was working on her homework. When Rose did so, she was better able to keep herself from becoming angry with Marcia.

A byproduct of fewer arguments was an overall improved relationship. Rose reported that she felt much closer to Marcia and that this feeling of closeness was put into words by Marcia's spontaneous comment one night as she was getting ready for bed. Rose said, "I was putting Marcia to bed when she turned to me and said, 'I love you mom'. She hasn't told me she loves me in the past year."

Leaving Living Room Messy

Sue is a single mother who complained that her son Tom, age fourteen, ignored her requests to keep the living room clean. Sue was asked to complete ABC reports to provide more information about this behavior.

Date: 1/12/08   Time of Day: 6:00 PM

1. What behavior did you see?

   __ fighting   __ running away   __ breaks things   __ tantrum

   X_ refusing to follow rules (describe: *Refuses to clean up living room*)

   __ aggression (describe) _____

   __ other_____

2. What happened immediately preceding Tom's negative behavior?

   __ school work (what?)_____

   X_ asked to do something (what? *Clean the living room*)

   __ asked not to do something (what?) _____

   __ told to stop doing something (what?) _____

3. Who was around when the behavior started?

   X_ mom   __ dad   __ sister   X_ brother   __ teacher   __ classmates   __ people in store

   __ other_____

4. Where was Tom when the behavior started?

   __ outside   __ classroom   __ kitchen   __ bedroom   X_ living room   __ in car

   __ grocery store   __ shopping   __ restaurant

__ other (where?) _____

__ other (where?) _____

5. What was the consequence of Tom's refusal to clean the living room?

__ taken from the room   __ spanked   __ sat in time out   <u>X</u> spoken to   __ left alone   __ grounded

Sue also talked of the context surrounding the disarrayed living room and Tom's refusal to clean it up. Sue worked all day and reported that when she returned home she would see popcorn strewn all over the living room floor, soda cans on the table, and crumbs from a half-eaten potato chip bag. When Sue confronted Tom, he blamed his brother for the mess. Mike also denied being responsible for the living room being a mess.

As is typical for most teenagers, Tom and Mike both enjoyed spending time with their friends on the weekends. Tom in particular wanted to go to a party Saturday night at his girlfriend's house. Mike also wanted to go skateboarding with his friends.

The therapist met with Sue, Tom, and Mike who agreed to the following contract:

Tom and Mike's Contract for the Weekend
2/26/08

By 5:30 PM Monday through Friday Mike and Tom agree that the living room will be straightened up — no food on the floor, soda cans in the garbage, and no potato chips or other food in the living room area. Tom is responsible for removing all food from the room, and Mike is responsible for removing all soda cans and drinks from the room by 5:30 PM.

Sue will check the room at 5:30 PM to confirm that it is clean for which both Tom and Mike earn the privilege to be with their friends. If the room is not clean as defined above, Tom and Mike will not be able to visit friends Saturday night but will have the opportunity to make another contract for the following week.

Signed,

_____   _____   _____
     Sue Smith   Tom Smith   Mike Smith

At the next session, Tom reported that he and his brother made sure that the room was cleaned by 5:30 each day. Both Tom and Mike noted that they enjoyed being with their friends. Tom's mother reported that she feared that she might not have been able to enforce the contract but she was resolved and ready to stick to the terms of the contract no matter what happened. It is this resolve that resulted in Tom and Mike changing their behavior. When parents cave in and don't enforce the stated consequences, the child translates whatever the parent says to: "No matter what my folks say, they won't follow through, so I can do as I please." Parents who teach their child that they will not follow through results in a child who will create a nightmare for parents to live in.

Looking at Internet Porn

A mother reported that her twelve-year-old son had been looking at "Asian pornography." She discovered his "pornography" behavior since she has a device on her computer which allows her to track all sites visited. Her shock was not than young male teens have an interest in pornography but that HER son was looking at pornography on the LIVING ROOM COMPUTER!

After building rapport with her via a session of reflective statements (e.g. "This is obviously upsetting to you"), the therapist asked her what her values were regarding pornography and what she felt she would like to do about her son's watching pornography. The mother noted that she did not like pornography, thought it was degrading to women, and she did not want her soon looking at it. The therapist acknowledged her value and told her while she had the goal of stopping her son from viewing pornography in the house, at best, she would be successful at suppressing the behavior on the computer but she could not stop him from sneaking sex books into the house (and to not be surprised if she found some later). "Males may be hard wired to derive pleasure from the visual stimulus of a naked female — indeed the survival of the species depends on it. If males were indifferent to female nudity, there would be no procreation, and the species would cease to exist."

The therapist also suggested that she not be overly critical of her son's interest in pornography so as not to associate sex with guilt. Instead, she might say, "I was going through the various sites that have been visited on the computer in the living room and noticed that an Asian pornography site has been visited. I know that teenage males are interested in this sort of thing but I don't feel comfortable with your looking at pornography on the home computer." The result was that the son felt embarrassed and did not visit a porno site again on the home computer.

As an aside, in general, parents should put the family computer in a conspicuous place such as the living room so that the teen will be less likely to look at sites parents will find objectionable. Parents can also install spyware, as this parent did, so that they can be aware of the various sites their teenager has been visiting.

Smoking Marijuana

A couple reported that they found a small bag of marijuana in their son's top drawer and asked what they should do. The therapist suggested that they make the son aware that they found the bag, that they could not condone its use, and to never bring it in the house or let them hear of it again. The implicit message is that they are not going to disown their son for marijuana use, that they do not approve, and to either stop it or keep it a secret. Most teens who use marijuana do so recreationally in a group context. It is rare that an adolescent will "stay stoned" all day, flunk out of school, and be unable to maintain a love relationship with a partner due to marijuana use.

Should excessive marijuana use and abuse be occurring, the teen should be seen alone by the therapist. It is most often the case that there are numerous other issues going on in the teen's life (rejection in relationships, low self esteem, poor relationship with parents, bad grades, etc.) that can be addressed by the therapist. The basic treatment plan is to enlist the aid of the teen in resolving the "other" issues which usually results is less need to "get high" to escape the array of negatives in the teen's life.

Smoking Cigarettes

Parents who become aware that their teen is smoking often become frantic. And for good reason. The negative health consequences of cigarettes are well documented. Nevertheless, teens smoke for two reasons: the nicotine is pleasurable (produces a high/is addictive) and cigarettes are often smoked by one's peers so a teen will smoke to be included in the group. Since most parents want their teen to stop smoking, the approach is direct. The teen is seen alone by the therapist to establish rapport which is needed when the teen meets with the parents to negotiate a non-cigarette-smoking contract. In effect, the parents make it clear that they want their teen to stop and are willing to do most anything to get it; in effect, the teen is asked to name his or her price: car, trip to the beach, whatever.

Such an approach maintains a positive relationship with the parents and has a higher chance of working than the parents' simply telling the teen to stop. Since the behavior is addictive, they will need the cooperation of the teen to stop. After the contract is negotiated, the therapist will ask the teen to keep records and to meet with the therapist. The result is usually very positive.

Drinking Alcohol

Alcohol is the drug most teens have experienced. Occasional limited recreational use of alcohol should be of little concern. Some European cultures socialize their youth to use alcohol conservatively by allowing teens to have a glass of wine at meals.

On the other hand, teens who come home drunk or hide alcohol in their rooms are engaging in behavior parents should not overlook. Not only is alcohol against the law for teenagers, drinking and driving can be deadly. Parents should not tolerate the latter and inform their teen that they can call the parent whenever and wherever to "come and get me" and that there will be no questions asked. While the parents do not approve of drinking, the goal is for the teen not to drink and drive. Most parents know of a parent whose son or daughter has had a serious alcohol-related accident. It is a behavior neither parents nor teens recover from — the house rule is no alcohol and driving.

Lying to Parents

As noted earlier, most teenagers report having lied to their parents at some time. Such lying should not be tolerated. One couple complained that their daughter was a "pathological" liar — that she lied about everything. Records revealed that the lying was mostly about being somewhere she wasn't supposed to be and being with someone she wasn't supposed to be with. The couple was instructed to always check up on where their daughter was and, if they found that she was not where she said she was to be or with whom she said she was to be with, they were to provide immediate consequences such as removing the phone, television, and computer from their daughter's room and forbidding her to use the house phone, the TV in the living room, and the family computer for a month.

During the next week, the daughter did, indeed, tell her parents that she was going to the library to study with her best friend. The parents went to the library to find her; she was not there. They called her best friend, who did not know where she was. The daughter was with her boyfriend (four years older than she was, no less) at his apartment. When the daughter came home and said she had a good time with her friend at the library, the parents followed through with the consequences, which stayed in place for a month. Thereafter, she was told that her next episode of lying would result in three months of consequences.

While the above program provided a negative consequence for lying, the parents were also told of the importance of complimenting their daughter for being where she said she would be. The daughter's lying to parents behavior dropped to zero.

Dating Someone Parents Disapprove Of

Parents are frequently aghast at the partners their teen selects to get involved with. Fathers, particularly, are concerned that their daughters date "bums" (e.g. guy has no job, no education, no ambition, tattoos, and metal on his face). One payoff for the daughter is to "get back at her parents" by dating someone her parents disapprove of. However, in some cases, a daughter may truly love a guy her parents find objectionable.

Restricting and prohibiting a daughter sometimes works. "You are not to see this guy. Dating him is off the list." While the daughter may, from the parents' point of view, have nothing to do with the guy, she may secretly be seeing him, doing drugs, and having sex with him. Love will find a way if the teens want to be together. However, research shows that if parents are adamant in their teen not being involved with someone, while the teen may "sneak around and see the guy," more often she ends up breaking up with the guy. "I'm not willing to give up the relationship with my parents over this guy," said one teen. Parents might be well advised to stay the course. The cost to the parents for prohibiting a love interest of their daughter is that the daughter will stay locked up in her room and won't speak to her parents. Her goal is to punish her parents for interfering in her relationship with her fellow. Again, parents need not be deterred but should keep the rule in place. In the long run, the daughter is likely not to end up with the guy her parents adamantly disapprove of.

An alternative strategy is for parents to register their opinion of a particular person (e.g. "we would rather you date someone else") but not to prohibit their teen from seeing the person. This parental response removes "I'll show you who's boss" from the agenda of the teen dating someone they do not approve of. In effect, there is no reinforcement value to the teen for dating someone her parents disapprove of since they said she could do so. In effect, the teen must find the PERSON reinforcing to continue to date the person. What often happens when parents tell a teen "date whom you want" is that the teen ends up dating people the parents find acceptable. The approval of parents does, indeed, matter.

There are occasions in which parents might well exercise all of their consequences against their teen dating someone they do not like. Most parents, particularly fathers, do not want their teen dating someone who is significantly older. For example a precocious sixteen-year-old who looks twenty-one will easily attract a twenty-five-year-old-guy. Research demonstrates that teen females who date significantly (e.g. five years or more) older guys end up having sex earlier than teens who date persons their own age. Simply prohibiting the behavior and close monitoring may help quell the relationship. However, parents should never be surprised to find out later whom their teen dated.

Sex

Parents may want their son or daughter to avoid having intercourse. Since most do so before graduating from high school, parents fear that their offspring will contract a sexually transmitted infection or get pregnant. The strategy of some parents is to never discuss the sexual issue in hopes that their son or daughter will assume that they (the parents) do not want them to engage in intercourse and comply. The strategy of other parents is to be very open with their teens, give them books like those earlier suggested, and be direct about protection against STIs and unwanted pregnancy.

In regard to protection from STIs, some parents buy condoms for their son or daughter, put them in a drawer in their own bedroom, tell the son or daughter to "help yourself," and instruct them that under no conditions are they to have intercourse without using a condom. In regard to pregnancy protection, some parents make it clear that they are willing to schedule an appointment with their daughter's physician to discuss with the daughter various birth control options. The function of being direct is to make the sexual issue visible and give the teen the protection to prevent both an STI and an unwanted pregnancy.

Chapter 6

Case Histories: Adolescents

Sound travels slowly. Sometimes the things you say when your kids
are teenagers don't reach them 'til they are in their forties.

Michael Hodgin

Case 1: Speeding

A couple who were being seen in marriage therapy complained that their sixteen-year-old had received two speeding tickets and been involved in an accident since they gave her a car six weeks ago. They were fearful that she would get into a serious accident. The therapist recommended to the parents that the teen: a. be required to attend a "safe driving" school, b. agree to drive the car no faster than 40 miles an hour until further notice, and c. not get another ticket for any reason. In the meantime, the teen would not be allowed to drive her car until completing the safe driving course.

Once the course was completed, the teen could drive. But, if she were seen driving above 40 miles an hour, the car would be kept at a friend of the parents and her driving privileges suspended for a year. The same consequences would also apply for getting a ticket from the police/highway patrol for any reason. The couple reported no incident in regard to driving safety on the part of their teen up to a year later when they were no longer seen in therapy.

Case 2: Failing to Return Borrowed Items

A father complained that his son would regularly borrow his fishing rods and hunting guns and not return them. The therapist recommended that the father remove his equipment to a closet in the father's bedroom and tell the son he could no longer borrow his equipment without asking. Once the son asked to borrow some equipment, the father was to loan it to his son with a specific date of return on which the son would put it back (after having cleaned it). Should the son not return the equipment (cleaned), the father was to suspend borrowing privileges for a year. The son did borrow the equipment, did not return it, and the father suspended his son's borrowing privileges. The father reported that his son was "mad at him" for not letting him borrow his equipment. The therapist suggested that teaching a son to return something he borrows is a worthy lesson and to apply the consequences as promised. The father dropped out of therapy so no additional information is available.

Case 3: Breaking Curfew

Parents of a sixteen year-old reported that their son would not respect the time that they gave him to return home. They did not want to keep him on a tight leash but they also felt that staying out 'til 2:00 AM was not acceptable. Furthermore, they feared that giving him a rigid time to be home would result in his speeding home to meet the deadline which could result in a serious accident.

The therapist suggested that the parents tell their son that staying out until 2:00 AM was unacceptable, was not to happen again, and that car privileges would be suspended for six months if he could not abide by the house rules. Furthermore, his growing up and making wise and mature decisions was important. Hence, while "around midnight" was the general expectation, there would be no hard and fast curfew time, but, that if he were not "reasonable" in deciding when to come home, he would not be allowed to drive the car for six weeks.

The intent of being vague about the time the teen was to be home was deliberate. Not only did it remove a time that might cause the teen to speed home (and be vulnerable to getting into an accident), the vague time created a context where the teen could begin to develop "wise" and "mature" decisions. Furthermore, a vague time might create internal anxiety once it became later than midnight.

The result was as desired. The parents noted that their son was reasonable and on most occasions did return home close to midnight. On no occasion was he later than 12:30 AM. The parents noted that they told their son that he was exercising good judgment and that they were proud of him.

Case 4: Piercings and Tattoos

A single mother complained that her seventeen-year-old daughter wanted to tattoo her face, arms and legs. She also wanted to get a pierced tongue ring and get her upper lip pierced and put a silver ring in it. Her mother was adamant about her daughter neither tattooing nor piercing her body. The therapist noted that tattoos and piercings are now part of the youth culture and some young people are just as adamant about having them. Since the mother said that "no freak is living in my house," the therapist recommended that the mother make clear to the daughter her preference and to back it up with consequences. Specifically, should the daughter get either a tattoo or a piercing that was visible (a tongue piercing was defined as visible), her phone, TV, and car privileges would be suspended indefinitely.

The daughter complied and got neither tattoo nor piercing during her senior year in high school. Since the daughter wanted to go to college, the mother told her that should she "mutilate" her body during college that she (the mother) would cut off her money. The daughter moved out, did not go to college, got a job, and got both tattoos and piercings (very visible). The relationship between the mother and the daughter became very strained. While the mother was heartbroken, she remained steadfast that she did the right thing in terms of cutting her daughter off.

This case illustrates two important points in therapy and in parenting teenagers/young adults. In regard to therapy, behavior change is possible only when consequences can be controlled. As long as the seventeen-year-old was living at home, the mother controlled some significant reinforcers (e.g. phone, TV, and car). Once the eighteen-year-old left home and became economically independent, the mother no longer had control of her daughter's reinforcers (who could do as she pleased).

The point for parenting teens and young adults is to be careful in selecting issues over which one is willing to end a relationship. For this mother, she would rather end the relationship with her daughter than be in the daughter's life if she were going to tattoo and pierce her body. As therapists, our role is not to be judgmental but to suggest to parents that sometimes a higher value might be maintaining the relationship with one's child over a specific issue such as tattoos/piercings. We have known parents who terminated the relationship with their son or daughter because the young adult was homosexual, married someone they did not like, or "left the church." Indeed Mennonite parents shun their children who leave the church. In effect, they no longer talk to or see them and the whole community is encouraged to have nothing to do with the "wayward" young adult.

In many cases, the youth return to the faith (for which they are rewarded not only by their parents, but the entire community).

Case 5: Failing Grades

Most parents are concerned that their children perform well in school. One couple reported that they were fearful that their son was going to flunk out of high school. Getting teens to study requires not only having a good relationship with them but being willing to devote time to monitoring their study behavior and to being consistent in providing appropriate consequences.

Since a student who is making an F in all subjects spends little time studying, parents should structure the environment of their teen. In the case of the parents mentioned above, this translated into specifying that they would drive their son to and from school (so there would be no lost time), go to school and get an agreement from each of his teachers to send a sheet home each day specifying what the homework for the evening was to be (to monitor specific homework performance), and set up consequences for his completing and not completing homework. For the son doing his homework nightly, his parents agreed that he would earn the right to use the phone, watch television, and play video games. For good reports from his teachers all week he could go out with his friends on the weekend. For not leaving school each afternoon with a note from each teacher on what homework he was to complete or for not completing these homework assignments each night, there would be no phone, no TV, no video game, and no leaving the house on weekends.

The parents reported fights with the son: He said that he didn't need to be treated like a baby, that he could drive himself to school, and that he could do as he pleased. The father informed him that to flunk out of high school was acting like a baby, that he (his dad) would drive him to school until the grades stabilized at a B, and that he could not do as he pleased. The father removed the phone and TV from the bedroom of the teen and told him he could get them back when he studied and provided the reports. The teen finally acquiesced to the structure and to the consequences, did finish high school, and is now in his first year of college.

Case 6: Having Friends Parents Do Not Like

Parents delight when their children select friends they (the parents) feel are a good influence on their son or daughter. In contrast, they react in horror when they see a friendship developing between their teen and someone they disapprove of. Max and Linda, parents of Brad, felt uneasy when they noticed that Brad was spending a lot of time with his new friend, Mike, who had dropped out of high school and who had been in trouble with the law. They were uncertain how to proceed — should they look the other way and let Brad pick his own friends or should they prohibit Brad from spending time with Mike?

The issue is complicated with advantages and disadvantages on both sides. The advantage of letting Brad pick his own friends is that there is no overt conflict with the parents. In addition, Brad learns to evaluate people himself rather than having his parents "screen" his relationships. Third, by not intervening in Brad's friendships, the parents would be showing confidence in his judgment thereby enhancing his self concept.

The downside of letting Brad develop a questionable friendship is the risk of negative modeling. Since Mike drinks daily, has dropped out of school, and has no interest in college, his behavior makes it easier for Brad to have a beer or two in the afternoons, let his studying slide, and think that college is a waste of time.

Brad's parents were fearful of the modeling effect of Mike on Brad and said to him "Mike is going nowhere" and "We only want you to associate with people 'going somewhere.' Dropping out of school, getting in trouble with the law, and making fun of college is 'nowhere.' We prefer you spend your time with other friends."

To say the least, Brad did not like his parents' interfering in his choice of friends. Only when he was told that he could not use the car to see Mike did Brad begin to spin up other friendships. While there was definite conflict between Brad and his parents, he eventually gave up Mike as a friend.

Another couple came to therapy with a similar concern. They took the position that, while they did not like it, they wanted their son to get experience selecting friends. The result was that their son felt that his parents "trusted" him and there was no conflict between the parents and the teen. And, two years later, their son no longer spent any time with the person they (the parents) had some reservations about.

Case 7: Refusing to Do Chores

Devin is fourteen. His parents recounted their frustration. "We have already tried everything we can think of to get him to do his chores. He eats in the kitchen and doesn't bother to clean up after himself. When he comes home, he goes straight to his room and plays his video games. When we tell him to take out the trash, he tells us that he's busy, or that he will get to it later, but never does. What should we do? We've already tried to take away his video games and he says he doesn't care. We've done everything we can think of to do."

Devin's parents were asked to identify Devin's likes. These included playing computer video games, spending time with friends, participating in church-youth activities, and listening to music. Recall our definition of a reinforcer in Chapter 1 — a reward is something that, when presented following a behavior, will increase the frequency of that behavior. A reinforcer can also be identified since its removal will also motivate behavior. If removal of an item, event, or activity does not motivate behavior, it is not a reinforcer, by definition. Devin's parents noted that Devin was not motivated by the withdrawal of video games. So, we conclude that while Devin seemingly enjoyed playing video games, he was not motivated to maintain his access to the games.

Devin's parents were asked to return the following week after paying particular attention to the things that he became angry about when he was denied access to them. They reported that he became angry when they would not let him go to his friend's house and when they would not "loan" him money to go to an after school activity. Bingo! We now had evidence that access to friends and money were reinforcers his parents could withhold to motivate his behavior. We would know for sure if he changed his behavior (did his chores) to get access to the reinforcers.

The new rules called for Devin's parents to cut off his allowance so that his only access to money would be from completing his chores (no work, no money). To make it clear how Devin could earn money, his mother devised a list of chores and provided behavioral specifics. For example, a "clean room" was one in which his shoes were in the closet, his bed was made, his socks/clothes in the hamper, and all of his other items would be where they belonged (basketball in the closet, video games on the desk next to the television, etc.). Cleaning the kitchen was defined as putting all dishes in the dishwasher, wiping the sinks and cabinets clean, and taking out the garbage. Mopping the floor would also involve removing the chairs to the next room, sweeping the floor, using a mild soap to mop the floor and rinsing the floor. He was also expected to return the cleaning items to the closet in the kitchen.

For keeping his room clean before he left for school and by noon on Saturday and Sunday, he was paid a dollar a day. For cleaning the kitchen on Saturday by noon, he was allowed to visit his friends Saturday evening.

Behavioral reports the following week revealed that Devin kept his room clean on five of seven days and that he cleaned the kitchen on Saturday. He was paid five dollars and allowed to go out Saturday night with his friends. Devin's parents were pleased with the outcome and said they no longer felt the need to attend therapy.

Case 8: Feeling Lonely

Rick was a fifteen-year-old going through a lot of changes in his life. He had been suspended twice and his grades were dropping. His parents were separated. His mother was distraught, had lost her job, and she could barely function. His dad had moved out but was preoccupied with his new girlfriend and working on his dissertation for his Ph.D. Friends at school had also begun to pick on Rick. He reported that he was very sad and lonely.

Rick was brought to therapy by his mother who reported, "I am concerned about him." Rick denied using any drugs or alcohol; he also denied suicidal thoughts or feelings. Rick also reiterated that he had been picked on in school. He described one friend he sat with at lunch, but otherwise, he did not have any friends. Additionally, he revealed that there was girl in his homeroom, Sandy, whom he wanted to introduce himself to and get to know. When the therapist asked, "What is your goal in our meeting here today; what would you like to happen in your life?" Rick made clear that he would like to have a relationship with Sandy but did not know how to go about it. After discussing with Rick the possibility of being rejected (and to be accepting of this), the therapist identified several alternative scripts for introducing himself and asking Sandy to join him for lunch:

Hey, Sandy, what are you having for lunch?

May I sit at your table?

May I join you for lunch?

May I sit here for lunch today?

In addition to the questions designed to get Sandy to agree that Rick could sit with her, the therapist suggested subjects that he could bring up with Sandy. Rick knew that Sandy had the same teacher that he had for English. He knew she played on the volleyball team and that she liked to play video games. The therapist and Rick role played, asking Sandy how she liked their English teacher, how long she had been playing volleyball, etc. The therapist also explained the difference between open- and close-ended questions and encouraged Rick to use the former. For example, "How do you like our English teacher?" is an **open-ended question** just as "Do you like our English teacher?" is a **closed-ended question**. The value of an open-ended question is that it requires the person to give more than a one-word response.

After identifying several potential phrases Rick might use to instigate a conversation with Sandy, Rick made the following agreement to approach Sandy at least once this week to ask if he could sit with her for lunch:

Agreement

I agree to approach Sandy at least once this week to ask if I may sit at her table or invite her to sit at mine. For doing this, the therapist will reduce my bill by five dollars. If I do not approach Sandy, there will be no reduction in the therapy bill, but I will have the opportunity to make another agreement the following week.

* * *

The following week, Rick reported that he had not approached Sandy at lunch but that he had done so after school in the courtyard asking her how her day was going and how her math test had gone. Although the approach behavior was not contracted for, the therapist did reinforce the Rick's assertive behavior. At last contact, Rick reported feeling greater comfort in initiating conversations and feeling less lonely.

Case 9: Being Disrespectful — A Therapeutic Failure

Bob and Aleta complained that their fifteen-year-old son, Tom, was refusing to help with chores, flunking out of high school, and had become aggressive in his temper outbursts to the point he would hit the wall with his fist which sometimes caused a hole in the wall. But their biggest complaint was disrespect.

Tom refused to speak to the therapist about the things that were happening in his house. He told his parents that he did not need to see a therapist. Tom's parents decided to continue going to therapy without Tom. Tom's mother described a tumultuous home where Tom felt free to come and go as he pleased. She said he had left home several times and stayed at a friend's house. Tom's mother said, "I'm tired of the way he always gets whatever he wants, it's like he thinks he runs the house."

Aleta was asked to describe a typical scenario with Tom. She replied, "He tells me to take him to his friend's house and if I don't, he becomes angry and calls me a bitch." At this point, she explained that the stepfather intervened and separated the mother and son. The stepfather noted, "I try to pull him aside and talk to him about what happened and see if I can help him calm down." Both parents agreed that when the son apologized, he was allowed to spend the night at his friend's house.

It became clear to Tom's parents that he had learned that when he did not get what he wanted from his mother through badgering her, he would try to work out a "deal" with his stepfather. In learning terms, Tom was reinforced for belittling his mother since some of the time she would give in. If not, he could talk his step-father into what he wanted.

The first goal of therapy was to bring the parents together in their resolve to foster a more cohesive parenting unit. Therapy focused upon the parents making decisions together. The therapist role played with the parents what they would do in situations where Tom tried to divide their authority. "I'll have to talk to Bob about this," Aleta would say, "Your father and I will have to talk about this before you can tell Jimmy you can spend the night at his house."

Beyond their willingness to tell the son they would check with the other before deciding what to do, the parents continued to disagree about what they expected of Tom and what consequences were appropriate. Bob said, "Tom is just being a boy and you are being too hard on him" while Aleta said to Bob, "You are too loosey-goosey and anything goes with you." The result is that the parents agreed on neither expectations nor consequences so Tom continued to be disrespectful. The couple dropped out of therapy.

Case 10: Sending Sexually Explicit Text Messages

The parents of fourteen-year-old Jennifer accidentally discovered that she was receiving sexually explicit text messages from a male peer. They talked with Jennifer about proper language and noted that these sexually explicit messages were not to be seen on her cell phone again and they were prohibiting her from using the cell phone or computer until further notice. Their concern, however, as presented to the therapist, was that Jennifer needed access to her cell phone since she was involved in a number of extra-curricular activities. They didn't want her to "get away" with having the sexually explicit text messages but they knew she needed the phone.

The therapist recommended that Jennifer be allowed to use her cell phone again. However, her parents would make regular checks to ensure that there were no inappropriate text messages. While these could be deleted, the frequency of the checks was such that it would be "risky" for Jennifer to be sending or receiving explicit sex text messages. Should the parents find such messages, Jennifer would lose the privilege of using her cell phone (and computer) for a month. Otherwise, she could continue to use her cell phone. The result was that the parents found no more sexual content in Jennifer's text messages.

Case 11: Managing Anxiety Attacks

"I get nervous and can't concentrate in class," complained thirteen-year-old Thomas as he described his anxiety attack. "I start worrying and my heart pounds." ABC reports revealed that the anxiety attacks occurred between three and four times per week.

The therapist showed Thomas how to tense and relax the various muscles of his body so as to induce relaxation. For example, Thomas would tighten his hand into a fist and hold tightly from two to five seconds and then relax. After repeating this sequence for three occasions, he would tense and relax his whole arm followed by the other hand and arm, etc. until he had relaxed his whole body.

Thomas made an agreement with the therapist to practice the relaxation exercise three times during the following week in exchange for a dollar from the therapist. The following week Thomas returned without having practiced at all. The therapist asked Thomas to lead him (the therapist) through a session of relaxation after which Thomas said that he would try to practice on his own the following week. The therapist asked if getting his parents to agree to let him have a friend spend the night on Friday night if he had practiced his relaxation exercises for three occasions that week would help to motivate him. Thomas said "yes" and returned the following week having practiced as agreed. The therapist recommended that he continue to practice the exercises three times a week. Six weeks later, Thomas reported he had not experienced any more panic attacks.

Case 12: Using Marbles as Tokens

Maxine and Ruby are the daughters of the first author and have been on a token system most of their lives. Although misbehavior does occur, there is a system in place that is a daily reminder for appropriate behavior. The system began with my wife and me identifying the behaviors we wanted our children to engage in. These became the "house rules" our children have grown up with.

Use kind words with each other.

Help the other sibling when asked.

Offer help to the other sibling spontaneously.

Read to the other sibling.

Play cooperatively with each other.

Use "quiet" voices in the house.

Be polite (e.g. say "yes sir," "thank you," and "please").

Put plate in sink after each meal.

Walk softly in house.

Vacuum the living room floor.

Pick clothes up off the floor.

Read chapters in books.

Practice musical instruments (fifteen minutes a day).

Offer to help parents with chores without being asked.

Sweep the kitchen.

Put clothes away without being asked.

Dust the furniture in the house.

Take out the trash.

For engaging in each of the above behaviors, each child earns a marble which can be redeemed for a reward she identified. Examples include:

Fifteen minutes of television viewing

Fifteen minutes of computer video game

Having a friend over

Each marble is also worth twenty-five cents which the child can redeem to buy an item on a school trip or something that the parents don't want to buy for them.

The result of this system is that, for the most part, the children engage in behaviors the parents value. It is important to note that because their parents value cooperative play and assistance of the older child with the younger child, parents pay particular attention to the times when the children play together. When they are "caught being good," parents reinforce the children saying, "Maxine, I am proud of the way you are playing with your sister, please have a marble." Parents offer the child an extra marble and the child knows exactly what she has done which earned the reward.

Case 13: Helping One's Child and an Entire Class*

Bob (a physician) and Mary are thirty-five years old, married, and the parents of a twelve-year-old son, Bill. They were seen for family therapy. At issue was the fact that Bill had specific learning disabilities in math and was entering middle school. Bob and Mary were concerned that the transition into middle school, and the changes associated with this, might place Bill farther behind in his math skills. They were more than happy to help with homework but, with changing math programs, they were not sure if they could be helpful to their son. Baseline data revealed that Bill was a very bright and intelligent child who was functioning about six months behind his grade level in math.

The intervention strategy: Bill had math as his first period in school from 7:40 AM to 8:25 AM. Since Bob had excelled in math and had expressed a commitment to keep his family first in the setting of a busy medical practice, he made a commitment to serve as a class aide for Bill in his first-period math class.

Bob realized that in order to be accepted in the best possible way in class, he needed to make his services available to all the students, not just Bill. He discussed this with the teacher and the teacher was initially cautious about the process. Bob suggested it was an empirical matter that they could try for two weeks, meet again to re-evaluate and if there were any concerns about his presence in the classroom, he would either change his behavior or not return. In those first two weeks, Bob realized there were a number of kids, primarily males,

* Case histories 13, 14 and 15 have been contributed by Robert Sammons, Jr. MD, Ph.D., a psychiatrist in Grand Junction, Colo., specializing in behavioral medicine.

the information before it was covered or could absorb enough by listening in class that he didn't have to do any studying. In inquiring further, it became clear that Jake had never developed any study skills and had come to believe that if he paid attention in class and heard the information one time, he would know the material. This notion was reinforced somewhat by his father who was an engineer and who had talked about being able to recall things from classes he took twenty years prior.

Jake's parents said that he had never been a behavior problem. He had been involved in very few fights at school and had never been sent to the principal for disciplinary action. They reported that as early as late fourth grade, his teachers began to state he was not working to his potential and those comments from teachers had continued. They said Jake's grades began to drop in the fifth grade and was more of a struggle than they thought it should have been. They were confused as to how he could have done so well in the early years of school, only to be doing so poorly now. They were baffled that their behavioral program was not working. To help understand Jake's situation, Jake's parents and teachers were given the Conner ADHD scale to complete. Their scores validated a diagnosis of Attention Deficit Hyperactivity Disorder.

The new intervention strategy involved placing Jake on Adderall XR 10 mg a day. His parents were asked to continue their behavioral program as the design (reinforcement followed study behavior) had no real weaknesses.

In returning two weeks later, Jake's parents reported the household was back to a fairly tranquil point. They had noticed a significant improvement in Jake's ability to sustain effort in studying and when they would quiz him on the material, his retention had improved. Jake said, initially, that he did not have the avoidance of studying he previously had. He was able to study at night and found that his ability to attend for a period of time had increased. He was completing his homework assignments at least on time and, on some occasions, would actually review the information twice. There had been a minimum of one grade level increase in his grades since beginning the medication.

Comment: Why is a medication case included in a chapter on behavioral intervention with children? There is an ever-increasing amount of literature which shows the beneficial effect of a combination of medication and behavioral interventions. Jake clearly had ADHD and although there is good literature to show that some children with ADHD can compensate for these difficulties with good behavioral programs, Jake's case represents a child who had a good program in place, but the ADHD prevented the program from working. Once Jake was placed on stimulant medication, that component of ADHD was brought under control. It is important to note that the therapist ensured the behavioral program continued.

What is frequently seen by therapists is that a program which did not work prior to the addition of medication worked extremely well once medication was begun. If medication worked so effectively, should behavioral intervention have continued? The answer is yes. There are clear benefits to behavioral interventions.

This case was also included because there are some behavioral therapists who are trained to proceed only with good behavioral intervention and are taught to be antagonistic toward the use of medication. This bias is supported frequently and loudly by opponents to medication throughout society. In spite of what some magazine articles and radio talk show hosts say, there is an overwhelming body of research supporting the biological nature of ADHD and its responsiveness to medication.

The treatment of ADHD from a biological perspective can be one of the most rewarding interventions that occur in medicine. Against the vast double-blind, placebo controlled research supporting the existence and treatment of ADHD with medication, there are case reports and anecdotal examples of a child doing poorly on medication or medication being inappropriately prescribed or misused by the patient or his family. Some call the antagonism to medication a "faith-based belief" as it is based upon a belief after hearing one story, reading one article or focusing only on the inevitable difficulties an occasional child will have (while ignoring the irrefutable research that is in contradiction to what they want to believe).

who either had Attention Deficit Disorder, learning disabilities, or were much more interested in the class than learning from it.

Using the contingency management skills Bob had learned, he asked the teacher if he could d Bob's Magic Club" in which he would have a card printed and would "engage in catching the stu good." This meant that any student could participate in the club, but he would particularly try to g disruptive students involved. He would show them a magic trick at the first of the week and once received five stars punched in his or her card, he would teach the trick to the child. Bob used some formed tricks, as well as more challenging tricks in order to motivate the students' interest.

Bob attended class 127 times, delaying the start of his rounds at the hospital and showing up ; an hour later. As a result of the father's involvement in the class, the students became less disrup dition, Bill's math skills came up to grade level and he received B's in math, a full grade higher tl mer year's performance. Over the course of the year, Bob had 27 different students involved in tl taught over 40 magic tricks. He said that, years later, the young men who were most often disrup would stop him on the street, ask if he remembered them and would tell Bob how much they magic and how good the class year was.

This case not only illustrates the value of a parent's front line help with his or her child but the efit to the entire class if the parent can offer contingent reinforcement (teaching magic tricks) for a study and classroom behavior.

Case 14: ADHD — Using Medication or Not

Jake was a twelve-year-old sixth-grader who was seen in therapy with his mother and father. were concerned that Jake was an underachiever and after initially doing quite well in school, h caught cheating on a spelling test. The parents had seen a behavioral specialist who assisted the fai ting on a contingency program where Jake's adherence to studying, turning in homework, and ma better in his grades were the target behavioral goals. In spite of this program, the couple had no cessful. They were referred with the hope I could evaluate their behavioral program and make rec tions.

In talking to Jake, he said he enjoyed school and enjoyed socializing with the other students. H that he was basically a popular guy and that the teachers liked him. He did not act out in class, was blemaker and did not disrupt class by talking or any other attention-getting behavior. He said he en of his classes but when it came to studying at night, he had a hard time doing so. He found othe more interesting and fun and even when placed on a good contingency program, he could only stud fifteen minutes at a time before becoming distracted by another project or activity in his room. S ties would occupy his time for twenty to thirty minutes. He tended to start studying but would no it. He rarely attended long enough to complete a chapter or an assignment. He said that when he ing, his mind would wander to what he would do after he finished a page or a section of homework. also think about what he would do the following day at recess or on the weekend with his friends.

When Jake was asked about his cheating, he said that school had been easy for him until fifth gra time he found that math became more difficult and he did not generally master a process before t was on to another concept. He had a cumulative effect of experiencing difficulty in math. In a simi said that memorizing words for spelling tests basically took more concentration than he could muste to please his parents and do well in school, he had started to cheat.

Jake was asked about his prior school behavior and he indicated he had been an excellent stud the top of his class for the first four years of school. He said school had come easily for him — he ei

Many parents are concerned about having their child on medication for fear that he or she will be labeled negatively. This concern belies the fact that if their child is not treated with appropriate medication, the child will continue to do poorly in school, may flunk out, may cheat, and receive a far more prejudicial label. The issue is not whether a child develops a "label" or not, but which label the child will be given. Untreated ADHD has a clearly recognized course which is certainly problematic for those who have a more disruptive condition.

Parents also fear that in this age of substance abuse, placing a child on stimulant medication increases the child's propensity for drug abuse. That, again, is a "faith-based belief" because the evidence is the opposite. When children are treated for their ADHD, they are much less likely to gravitate toward, or be grouped with, children who are poor performers and begin engaging in counter-culture activities to give them success in an area.

Research-based clinicians are not threatened by, nor antagonistic to, medical treatment of the behaviors they are trying to treat. A comprehensive whole person view is often necessary for the most robust treatment response. This is not a turf war regarding whose treatment is more powerful or more important. Rather, it is a team approach to afford the patient/client the most efficacious treatment available to him or her. The importance of a good behavioral analysis and program cannot be underestimated.

Case 15: Father Developing Relationship with Daughters

Jeff is a thirty-year-old married professional with two young girls. His concern was that he was the oldest of five children, had been active in a number of activities and had "never played a sport for which the letting of blood was not required." With two young girls, he was concerned about how to develop a relationship with them such that that they would not be interested in the same rough-and-tumble activities he enjoyed.

Jeff also did not want to follow the model of his father who had been a physician. His dad had complained that the only way he could get away from the office or emergency room was to either to go fishing or hunting. Jeff described his father as getting him up at 5:30 AM, going out on a hot Arkansas River, fishing until 8:30 PM and catching three fish. He said his father thought he had experienced the best day ever and Jeff thought his father was the dumbest man he had ever met. In essence, Jeff said the reinforcement frequency was too low (three bream in thirteen hours) and his father's unrealistic enthusiasm for the activities had completely extinguished Jeff's interest in hunting or fishing. He did not engage in either of these activities away from his father.

To avoid his father's mistake, Jeff said that he did not want to subject his daughters to prolonged exposure to activities they did not enjoy. But the result was that he did very little with them and he felt emotionally distant from them.

The behavioral goal was to develop activities that were reinforcing to Jeff and his daughters. Baseline data revealed that Jeff was willing to engage in activities with his daughters in which they shared mutual enjoyment. Currently, he would read to them frequently in the evening, choosing a series that was both interesting and age-appropriate to his girls, as well as being interesting to him. But he wanted more involvement.

The strategy was for Jeff to monitor his daughters' activities and whenever they showed an interest in an area which was of mild to moderate interest to him, he was to participate in that activity with his daughters. The goal would be less mastery of a particular activity but, rather, making it a fun and enjoyable activity for them.

In implementing this strategy, his oldest daughter asked for some magic tricks for her birthday. There was a store that sold a few magic items and he consulted a local magician about which items he should purchase. He also had the magician attend his daughter's birthday party, perform some magic and then do a teaching session where she learned to perform some magic tricks herself.

Over time, his daughter continued her interest in magic. When they would go to a larger town, Jeff would take his daughter to various magic shops and they would find age- and skill-appropriate tricks for her. Jeff found that he was able to become reacquainted and to enjoy the magic he had enjoyed as a young child, and the time he shared with his daughter became mutually enjoyable.

His other daughter evidenced an interest in learning various dancing steps. Jeff attacked her interest with the same vigor and hired a coach to teach her various steps. In her youth, they went to various father-daughter square dances. In effect, he bonded with both his daughters.

Chapter 7

Behavioral Marriage Therapy

Spouses are students and teachers of each other.

Neil Jacobson

In Chapter 1 we noted the importance of the therapist focusing not only on the parent-child relationship but the husband-wife relationship. By ensuring good marriage, the children grow up in a loving, nurturing, consistent context. For the therapist not to give time to the couple's marriage is to leave unattended the most important social context in the lives of their children.

Spouses feel happy or sad as a result of the behaviors their partners engage in. Positive behavior engenders feelings of love and intimacy whereas negative behavior results in anger and emotional distance. But whether positive or negative behavior, behavior is learned. The behavioral marriage counselor identifies the behaviors each spouse would like the other to engage in and, using the principles of learning, structures the spouse's interaction so that the desirable behaviors occur. Once these behaviors begin and negative behaviors are eliminated, the spouses have a more positive basis on which to feel better about each other.

Assumptions of Behavioral Marriage Therapy

The behavioral marriage therapist makes three assumptions: attitudes and feelings are based on behavior, behavior is learned, and behavior can change.

Attitudes and Feelings Are Based on Behavior

The way spouses feel about each other is based on the behavior the spouses engage in toward each other. Spouses bring to therapy feelings which are tied to negative behaviors on the part of their partners. These are identified and replaced with new behaviors to create new feelings.

Presenting Feeling	Behavior of Spouse	New Behavior	New Feeling
Sadness/Frustration	Avoidance/Neglect	Attention/Time	Love
Anger	Affair	End Affair/Fidelity	Happiness

Behavior Is Learned

In Chapter 1 on Behavioral Family Therapy we identified the four rules of learning. Here we give examples of how these rules can be used to understand marital interaction.

a. **Reward Rule.** Recall that this rule says that those behaviors followed by a positive consequence will increase. A spouse who calls when he or she is going to be late has been rewarded for doing so by "thanks for calling, Honey . . . I'll see you soon." A spouse who initiates sex has been rewarded for doing so. A spouse who is honest has been rewarded for honesty by the partner.

b. **Punishment Rule.** Recall that this rule says that behaviors followed by negative consequences will decrease. A spouse who does not call home when late has been punished for calling by "For Christ's sake . . . you are always late and I'm sick of it . . . (click)." A spouse who does not initiate sex feels either rejected by the partner or does not enjoy the sex that occurs. A spouse who lies has been punished for telling the truth. For example, a partner who revealed, "Yes, I have thought about having sex with your sister" and met with "You are despicable," will learn to keep these thoughts inside.

c. **Negative Reinforcement Rule.** Recall that when a person engages in a behavior that stops something negative, the behavior will be repeated. The husband takes out the garbage to stop his wife from nagging about it. The wife tells her husband it is fine for him to go golfing or fishing because she is tired of hearing him whine that he never has time to golf/fish any more.

d. **Extinction Rule.** Recall that when a behavior is no longer reinforced, the behavior will stop. Spouses stop talking with each other since doing so is no longer rewarding. Spouses have sex less often over time since they are always available to each other and the electricity of new sex is impossible to maintain over fifty years.

Behavior Can Change

Any behavior that can be learned can be unlearned and replaced with positive behavior. Spouses who criticize each other, demand, and don't spend time together can learn to compliment, negotiate, and enjoy being together. What has been true of a couple and their relationship need not be true for the future.

Goals of Behavioral Marriage Therapy

The behavioral marriage therapist has four goals in mind. These are in reference to focusing on behavior, focusing on positive behavior to increase, focusing on future behavior, and focusing on behaviors of both spouses.

Identify Behavior Each Spouse Wants the Other to Engage In

The behaviorist is continually translating what spouses say into concrete behavioral terms. The classic example is a wife who said, "I want my husband to be more 'considerate.'" Of course, this term means nothing so the wife was asked, "What does 'considerate' mean?" She responded, "You know, be nice." Since being "nice" is as vague a term as "considerate," the question followed, "What is an example of 'being considerate'?" The wife finally "got it" and responded, "You know, we'll be watching TV and he'll get up and go into the kitchen and fix himself a Skippy peanut butter and jelly sandwich and come back to the living room and sit down." Now we (as therapists) know what inconsiderate behavior is. But more importantly we know what "considerate" behavior is: "asking the spouse before going into the kitchen 'can I get you something from the kitchen'?" This request becomes a behavioral goal for the husband to engage in to show his wife that he is "considerate."

Emphasize Positive Behaviors to Increase
(Not Negative Behaviors to Decrease)

The behaviorist is also careful to focus on positive behaviors to increase rather than negative behaviors to decrease. Rather than the wife saying to the husband, "Stop being inconsiderate," it is important that she express what she wants in terms of future positive behavior: "When you go to the kitchen during a commercial, please ask me if you can bring me anything." Other examples include, "Start being on time" (defined as being present at the agreed upon time) rather than "Stop being late," "Limit your drinking at the party to two glasses of wine" rather than "Stop getting drunk," and "Take the kids to McDonald's Saturday morning" rather than "Stop being the absentee father you are with the kids."

Focus on Future Behaviors

While listening to the history of a couple's relationship is important for rapport building, future behavior is the focus of the behavior therapist. The therapist does not spend an endless number of sessions trying to "understand" a problem or to develop "insight" (since insight often does *not* translate into behavior change). Rather, the therapist wants to know what new behaviors the partners want each other to engage in this afternoon, tonight, tomorrow, etc. For example, while the history of an affair, "insight" into why it occurred, and the feelings of the respective partners are relevant content for the beginning of the first session, by the end of the session, the behavioral therapist will move the spouses toward no longer talking about the affair (neither spouse is to talk about the affair and to leave the room if the other one brings it up) and doing things each would like the other to do. The focus of therapy is not the past (about which nothing can be done), but the future (about which everything can be done).

Target New Behaviors of BOTH Spouses

Each session involves what each spouse can do for the other to make their relationship happier and more enjoyable. Spouses sometimes present to the therapist that "one of them is the problem and one of them needs to be fixed." "She had the affair," "He works too much," and "He spends too much time at his mother's" all suggest that there is one bad and one good spouse (the one who didn't have the affair, works too hard, etc.). As noted earlier, the behavior therapist conceptualizes the couple's relationship as one in which each provides rewards and punishments for the other which will affect their respective behaviors. If "she" had the affair, it is likely that he was not emotionally engaged with her so that she sought attention elsewhere. Hence, the focus of therapy is as much about her husband's behavior as a spouse and lover as about her being faithful.

Similarly, if "he" works too much, it is likely that his wife may not be very reinforcing (e.g. her focus is her work, her kids, and her parents). Notice that it is always the "busy" spouse who finds time for an affair. Hence the focus is on the relationship between the partners and the degree to which they are reinforcers for each other, not on one of them working too much. Similarly, if she spends all of her time in reference to her job, kids, and parents, we know that he has a low value as a reinforcer. The result is that the therapist must get each spouse to identify what they would like each other to do so that they are reinforcers for each other.

Behavior Contracts for Couples

The primary tool of the behavior therapist working with couples is the **behavior contract** — a document specifying the behaviors the spouse has agreed to perform during the next seven days and a line for the spouse to check each day to confirm that the behavior occurred. An example of a behavior contract for a husband follows:

Name: E. Fred	Mon.	Tues.	Wed.	Thurs.	Fri.	Sat.	Sun.
1. Two compliments to spouse each day	__	__	__	__	__	__	__
2. Ask spouse on Wed. for Sat. night date	__	__	__	__	__	__	__
3. Arrange for baby sitter for Saturday night	__	__	__	__	__	__	__
4. Set up lunch date with spouse once weekly	__	__	__	__	__	__	__
5. No negative statements to spouse	__	__	__	__	__	__	__

The first behavior specified in the sample contract is what the wife said she wanted her husband to do to please her. For example, the wife said, "He criticizes me all the time and never says anything good about me. I'd like for him to say something positive now and then."

The second item on the contract, "Ask spouse on Wednesday for Saturday night date" resulted from a conversation where the wife said, "My spouse never asks me to do anything fun — all we do is sit around the house." Hence, the husband is to ask his wife on Wednesday to go out on a date the following Saturday night. For item number three, the wife complained that "I always have to be responsible for getting a baby sitter — I'd like for him to get the baby sitter for when we go out." Hence, the husband's behavior contract includes that he takes responsibility for getting the baby sitter. Item four resulted from the wife saying, "I never see him during the week. He's always too busy." So the behavior for the husband is to initiate lunch with his wife once each week. For item five, the wife said, "I'm sick of him nagging me." So the behavior for the husband is to make no negative statements to his wife.

While we have provided an example of a behavior contract for the husband, the therapist would also develop one for the wife. Hence, the therapist would ask the husband what he wanted his wife to do to please him. Based on his answers, another behavior contract would be developed for the wife so that both spouses would leave the session with five specific behaviors each was to engage in for the other.

Hence, most spouses come to therapy with the same goal — to be happy. They tell the therapist what their partner is doing which makes them unhappy (e.g. "always nags and never asks me to go out"). In effect, the therapist identifies what behavior each spouse is currently engaging in which results in their partner not being happy — criticizing the other, not spending time together, and not complimenting each other — and translates these negative behaviors into positive behavioral specifics as reflected in the contract. The spouses are also asked to keep a record of the new behavior they have agreed to engage in so that the therapist will know that the spouses are doing what they agreed to do.

As noted, at the end of the first session, each spouse will leave with a behavior contract in his or her hand specifying what behaviors each is to engage in during the next week. To provide background for the clients to understand the use of behavior contracts the therapist says something like:

> *Let me suggest a way for you to think about your relationship. Both of you are obviously unhappy with the way things are going. These feelings do not come out of nowhere but are a result of specific behaviors each of you now engages in — you rarely compliment each other, criticize each other, and don't spend any time together. During this session each of you has identified what you would like each other to do to make you feel better about your partner: have your partner say nice things to you, stop criticizing/nagging you and initiate time to be alone with you on a "date." To ensure that these new behaviors actually occur, I have written them down on a sheet which I am giving to each of you. Please take this contract with you, check each day when you have done what you agreed to do and return this next week. Indeed, the first question I will ask when I see you next week is, "May I see your records please?"*

Criticisms of Behavioral Marriage Therapy

Behavior therapy is sometimes the target of criticism from both professionals and clients.

Professional Criticisms

1. "A behavioral approach does not treat the 'real' problem." Psychodynamic- and insight-oriented therapists suggest to behavior therapists that by focusing on behavior, they may not be dealing with the "real prob-

lem." For example, they may say that getting spouses to compliment each other and stop nagging each other does not deal with deep feelings of resentment, anger, and frustration. Indeed, this may be true. But the behavior therapist elects to focus on getting new positive behavior occurring now rather than take a chance that discussing past sources of rage for six sessions will result in new ways of relating to each other. Such discussions keep the therapist mired in a swamp of nowhere while his clients continue their same negative behavior. Indeed, there is little evidence that "insight" results in behavior change. Smokers have "insight" that smoking is dangerous for their health but continue smoking since nicotine is reinforcing. Identifying specific behavior that each partner wants the other to engage in and sending clients home with behavior contracts offers new hope for feeling different — now.

The behavior therapist believes that clients can "act themselves into a new way of thinking, quicker than they can think themselves into a new way of acting." Once spouses begin to compliment each other, stop criticizing each other and go out on "dates," they have a new basis on which to feel more positively about each other. If no new behavior is begun, there is no new basis for a change in attitudes and feelings.

2. "A behavioral approach is cold and inhumane." A classic book, *Science of Human Behavior* by B.F. Skinner, details how behavior is learned and can be changed. Behavior therapists recognize just as bringing science to bear on relationships is important, it is equally important to present the science humanely so that it is a "humane science." Indeed, not to systematically address the feelings of clients, identify behavioral causes, and initiate new behaviors to create new feelings would be most inhumane. Behavior therapists also recognize the importance of rapport with clients. If clients do not like the therapist (e.g. do not perceive him or her as a reinforcer) his or her influence will be zero in terms of being motivated to follow through with behavior contracts.

Not long ago, the second author was on a runway for two hours in Dallas. The pilot apologized for the delay and said booze was going to be made available to turn the airplane into a "flying saloon." The passengers cheered. In effect, the pilot was being "humane" by recognizing the frustration of being delayed in taking off. But the pilot's being "humane" would not be enough. The passengers also wanted their pilot to be very scientific about airspeed, liftoff, and touchdown. One without the other is not as good as both. The behaviorist is humane in terms of feeling empathy for the interpersonal pain and frustration of his or her clients but is scientific in terms of delivering the goods for behavior change which will help alleviate the suffering.

Lay Person Criticisms

1. "Spouse in a box." As noted earlier in this chapter, the behavior therapist will ask each spouse to engage in new behavior for the other. These behaviors are often very personal and intimate such as saying, "I love you," initiating affection (hug), or initiating intercourse.

Sometimes a spouse will say, "I want my partner to hug me and ask me to go out Saturday night because my spouse wants to, not because you wrote it down on one of these silly contracts." Our response as therapists is that we understand the desire for the behavior to come from the heart of the partner. And, indeed it is, in that that the spouse has a CHOICE about whether to please the partner. He or she could certainly say "I don't care what my spouse thinks or feels and I'm not doing anything to make things better. If you have to work at a marriage, it's not worth having." Of course, this position means the marriage is over (but is not likely since couples who come for marriage counseling are usually motivated to do things to improve the relationship).

In addition, the therapist points out the concept of "spouse in a box." In effect, the partner who says, "I want my partner to tell me I am loved and to hug me" and when the partner engages in this behavior, takes the position that "My partner is doing this for the wrong reason — just because the therapist says so" has the spouse "in a box." The partner can either engage in the behavior or not — but if the partner engages in the behavior, but for the "wrong" reason, the spouse can't win. The way to let the spouse out of the box is to for the spouse to acknowledge the CHOICE his or her partner is making to do things for the partner.

2. "Too much structure." Clients sometimes complain that "there is too much structure" and they are resistant to using behavior contracts and keeping records. We respond by making a deal — to do it the clients' way the first week and revert to structure the second week if they do not experience the desired behavioral and feeling changes. In effect, the clients agree to do the things the therapist recommends (based on what the clients identified as their goals) and to report the following week "how things went." If they did not do what they agreed to do, the therapist asks them to either change their goal (e.g. improving their relationship is not important) or to use the behavior contracts (e.g. keep a record of the new behaviors they engage in).

Ten Tricks of the Trade for Marriage Therapists

There are ten tricks of the trade for treating couples.

See the Husband and Wife Together

A critical mistake of psychologists is that they see the spouses alone. Doing so is productive for working on individual problems. However, marriage is defined by *interaction* so spouses must be seen together to manage the *relationship*. Of course, there are occasions when one spouse calls for an appointment and is not sure if he or she wants to continue the relationship. In such a case, the therapist encourages the client to consider improving the marriage, which means involving the spouse. The reason for nudging the spouse toward working on the marriage is the implied motivation on the part of the client who scheduled the appointment with a therapist to "talk about the marriage." If the spouse were confirmed in his or her decision to end the marriage, he or she would have called an attorney!

Once a decision is made to involve the spouse, the therapist asks the partner to have his or her mate call to schedule an individual session. All marriages have two points of view and the therapist must hear both points of view independently. Otherwise, if the therapist sees the couple the next session, the "other" spouse feels that he or she is coming into a context where the therapist is already biased against him or her.

Stay Neutral

The effect of seeing both spouses an equal amount of time (if one is seen separately, the other must also be seen) and together on a regular basis is to keep the therapist neutral. This posture must continually be maintained throughout the therapy. While the therapist will have biases, each spouse must be viewed as having a legitimate point of view. If the therapist is viewed as "siding" with one spouse, the effectiveness of working with the couple will drop to zero.

Keep Rapport High

While the behavior therapist is very focused on identifying what each partner would like the other to do, setting up behavior contracts, etc., he or she will also take time to "hear" the story of each partner to learn what it is like to feel each partner's point of view. A high frequency of reflective statements ("So you feel devastated to learn that your partner has become involved with someone on the Internet") is critical to developing such rapport. If you lose rapport with your clients, you've lost your couple and they won't be back.

Focus on Least Motivated Spouse

Spouses are usually not equally motivated. Rather, one is usually the impetus for the other being in the therapy room. The therapist must quickly identify the **least motivated spouse** and spend 80 percent of the first session focused on the needs of this spouse. While it is clear that the highly motivated spouse will return to therapy next week, the therapist has one shot at making the therapeutic context rewarding enough for the least motivated spouse to want to return. The mechanism for ensuring this return is to simply ask this spouse "What is the relationship like from your point of view?" "How are you feeling about things?" "What would you like your partner to do to make things better for you?" The answers will result in a list of behaviors this spouse would like the other to do. The therapist then turns to the highly motivated spouse to assess his or her willingness to do as requested. Since this is the most motivated spouse, he or she is usually most willing to agree to do as requested. The result is that the least motivated spouse quickly learns "when I come to therapy, I leave with my spouse agreeing to do stuff I want. This (therapy) is a place I want to return to." Bingo!

Have Couples Complete the Marriage Inventory

Once an appointment is made, the therapist may mail the spouses the **Marriage Inventory** (see Chapter 10) which they are to complete and mail to the therapist before the first session. This inventory saves a great deal of time, allows the couple to provide the therapist with their important concerns, and focuses the therapist during the first session.

Avoid Working on Sex and Money First

The last page of the Marriage Inventory asks the respective spouses, "What would you like to work on first?" While their answer will provide a general guideline for a starting point, the therapist will need to exercise his or her judgment. "Sex" and "money" are always to be avoided as "first" problems to work on. Since both are tied to the larger relationship issues of closeness, intimacy, affection, and communication, any therapist will be doomed by focusing on sex or money first.

Should spouses specify sex as the issue they want to work on first, the therapist might say:

> *I appreciate your identifying what you would like to work on first when we are together. Both of you listed "sex" and I guarantee that will be the priority. But we can't attack the issue directly. As you know, how you feel about each other, your level of intimacy, communication, etc. very much affect your sexual relationship. So let me move back a moment to your out-of-bed relationship and ask how you two are doing, how you feel about each other, how you spend your leisure time, how you communicate? These issues will affect your sexual relationship.*

Similarly, couples who elect "money" as the issue they would like to work on first are told:

> *I appreciate your identifying what you would like to work on first when we are together. Both of you listed "money" and I guarantee that will be the priority. But we can't attack the money issue directly. As you know, how you feel about each other, your level of intimacy, communication, etc. very much affect how you manage money in your relationship. Money is about power and control and when you are feeling good about each other, you are much less apt to argue over money than when you haven't spoken for a week. So let me begin by asking how you two are doing, how you feel about each other, how you spend your leisure time, how you communicate? These issues will affect your economic relationship.*

Work on High Frequency Behaviors First

In addition to avoiding sex and money as the focus of the first or second session of therapy, it is important to select behaviors which occur frequently in the relationship. The classic example is a couple who spent twenty minutes talking about a mother-in-law and how intrusive she was. After using the twenty minutes to build rapport, the second author asked, "How often does your mother-in-law visit?" "Every summer for a week," was the reply. Since this session was in September, the goal was to shift the attention to behaviors that happen daily or weekly in the relationship — frequency of positive statements each makes to the other daily, frequency of critical or negative remarks each makes to the other daily, and how often the couple go out alone on a weekly basis (without the kids) for dinner, etc. are behaviors worthy of focus.

Cognitions Are Crucial

Cognitive behavioral therapy is an important subspecialty of behavioral therapy. "Cognition" is another word for "thought" and how spouses think about a situation has a definite effect on how the spouse behaves. A spouse who has the thought, "my partner is hot and open for sex" will likely initiate sex while one who perceives the partner as "cold and uninterested" will be less likely to do so.

Another example of the power of one's cognitions may be instructive. A husband complained that his wife kept the house an absolute cluttered wreck with her "frigging coupons." He noted that there were boxes "stacked high everywhere in the house" and that he had to walk "sideways" half the time to navigate where he was going. The wife admitted that she loved clipping coupons and that she saved the family a great deal of money. The husband was not convinced and viewed the coupons as a "mountain of junk."

To get more information, the therapist asked the wife to take the husband to the grocery store to buy the items they needed for a week. After filling the grocery cart to the brim which included the husband's beer and nachos, the clerk announced $138.16. The wife then looked in her "coupon" satchel and began to take out coupon after coupon. After the clerk added up the value of all of her coupons, the new total for the groceries was $18 and some change. The husband was in shock at the amount of money the coupons were worth and changed his view of the "clutter of junk" to "boxes of money" (and the more the better).

The point for therapy is that it is important to identify what cognitions are operative and to investigate the ease and value of changing them. This book has been about behavior change. However, sometimes it is easier to change a cognition than a behavior. In the example of the coupons, we have two options for the disgruntled husband — get his wife to "clean up the clutter/boxes" or get him to change his view of the boxes. Either alternative gets the couple to the same goal — they are no longer fighting about boxes in the house.

Similarly, a spouse may get upset that his partner's parents are visiting for a week. But to change the cognition of their coming and their being there, the couple may agree on an exchange which provides a new cognition for the partner. For example, a wife wanted her parents to visit for a week, which was viewed by the husband as a week he would need to tolerate his in-laws being in the house. She asked the husband what he would like for her to do for him and he said "fly fishing in West Virginia." They agreed that the week after her parents were to visit that the wife would go fly fishing with her husband in West Virginia. Rather than brood about his in-laws coming or being miserable with them in the house for a week, the husband now had a new cognition — fly fishing with his wife in West Virginia.

Some Problems May Be Individual Rather Than Marital

Sometimes spouses identify problems they would like to work on in therapy that are specific to them as individuals rather than them as a couple. Depending on the training and skills of the therapist, some of these may be appropriate for the therapist to work on while others would not be appropriate. Problems related to losing weight and alcohol/drug abuse are clearly individual issues which only therapists who specialize in these areas should treat. Psychologists are more likely to have such expertise than marriage/family therapists or social workers.

On the other hand, problems related to one's self concept/self image, which may impact the marriage indirectly, may be issues the therapist feels comfortable treating. When a **positive self concept** is defined as a high frequency of positive self referent statements and a **negative self concept** is defined as a low frequency of positive self referent statements, the behavior therapist can move forward. This involves having the client make a list of ten positives about himself or herself and writing them on a 3x5 card. These positives may be generated by the client asking the spouse and close friends to identify their top qualities. If the client agrees that the quality identified by the friend is, indeed, a positive, it goes on the list. The client then systematically looks at this 3x5 card several times a day and repeats to himself or herself one's positive qualities. The late Dr. Jack Turner developed this exercise known as **Dr. Turner's Dr. Pepper Game** whereby the client at ten, two and four whips out the card of positives and reads it (Dr. Pepper's advertising campaign in the '50s was to drink Dr. Pepper at ten, two, and four). In practice, the intervals should be spaced wider apart such as nine, three, and nine.

Be Attentive to Client Compliance

As noted in Chapter 2 on Assessment, having clients engage in the requested behavior of keeping records and following through with behavior contracts is an issue of compliant behavior which is enhanced with strong rapport and reinforcement by the therapist. Thanking the clients for showing up on time, bringing their records, and doing what they agreed to do is important in increasing the frequency with which clients are compliant. Clients do not improve in therapy unless they engage in new behavior and new behavior does not occur unless the client views the therapist as a reinforcer and engages in the new behavior identified by the therapist. Reinforcing the clients for what they do cannot be overemphasized.

Communication Basics for Spouses

Parents are communication models for their children. The way they interact with each other teaches the children the norms of family communication and how they may interact with their parents. If parents yell and scream at each other, the children are more likely to yell and scream at their parents. If parents model the behavior of respect for each other and for their children, the children will learn similar norms of communication with their parents.

In effect, parents set the communication tone of the family. The following are communication basics for the therapist to encourage his or clients to integrate into their relationship.

Compliment Frequently

Spouses never tire of hearing good things said to and about them. Just as the spouses said in courtship, "You look terrific," "It is wonderful to be sharing this life with you," and "You did a great job," it is important that spouses continue frequent compliments to each other. Indeed, notice that the sample behavior contract provided earlier in the chapter specified that the husband make two positive statements to his wife each day. "Thank you for picking up the milk on the way home," "Thanks for putting gas in the car," and "You look great," are examples.

Compliment the Spouse in Front of Others

In addition to saying good things to each other in private, there is an added value for spouses complimenting each other when with others. Bragging about each other, telling others what a great cook or punctual or responsible partner the spouse is sends sweetness into the marital/family air. The spouses not only bask in the delight of each other but in the smiles of friends who smirk and roll their eyes in disbelief. Of course, the spouses might also compliment their children in public so that their children hear them say good things about them to their friends.

Make Words and Body Language Congruent

Messages are most clear when the spouses' words match their body language. Saying "Okay, you're right" accompanied by a smile and an embrace reflects using both words and body language to convey the same message. In contrast, saying "OK, you're right" but leaving the room and slamming the door communicate a very different message. Spouses need to ensure that what they say and their body language convey the same message. The message to children is to be consistent with their words and behavior. Hollering and slamming doors is never appropriate no matter how much they say they love their parents.

Gripe Productively

A key element of communication between spouses is the emotional connection. **Communication** is not talking about the weather but talking about the delight in being with each other, making plans for future fun times, and yes, telling each other what he or she would like the other to do to enhance life with each other. A modest degree of fault-finding between spouses is functional — the partners remain realistic about themselves and their relationship and, by doing so, keep the relationship on course and in orbit. By listening to and airing each other's critical thoughts, the spouses alert each other to behavioral changes each would like for the other to begin. Not all gripe sessions will result neatly in "OK, Honey, I'll be glad to do that — anything else?" but they keep the marital air fresh and clean. Spouses who don't air their gripes hide their resentment which often surfaces elsewhere — not talking, less intimacy, less sex.

But griping must be the right kind. **Productive griping** requires that each spouse make clear specific future positive behavior he or she would like the other to engage in. These conversations give the partners a roadmap of what to do to keep their partner happy. **Destructive griping** is a useless harangue; it leaves the spouses depressed and resentful since their partner just unloaded on them but did not specify what new behaviors they wanted to see. Some examples of productive and destructive griping follow:

Productive Griping	*Destructive Griping*
"Please leave the gas tank at least a quarter full when you take the car out."	"You are always inconsiderate. You always bring the car home on empty."
"Please be on time when we plan to meet someplace or call me if you are going to be late."	"You can't be depended on for anything. You are chronically late and don't care about my feelings."
"Please clean up the kitchen on Saturdays before noon."	"You think I am your maid and cook and you never help me do anything."

Focus on Future

As noted earlier, notice that each of the above items under the "productive griping" column is specific to a behavior in the future. The spouses should be encouraged not to drone on about past behavior that is upsetting but to focus on what they want to happen in the future. Not only are their gripes to be future focused (something the partner can change), they are to be behaviorally specific. Asking the partner to "respect me" is not behaviorally specific and relies on the partner to guess what to do. Being asked to leave a half of tank of gas in the car, be on time, and clean the kitchen are clear.

Keep the Process of Communication Going

Communication is both content and process. While **content** is the word spouses use, **process** is the interaction between the partners. It is important that spouses not be discouraged by difficult content so that one or both shuts down and stomps out of the room. The therapist might say something like the following:

> *When your partner tells you that you did something that upset him or her, it can be upsetting for you to hear this. But the advantage of your partner telling you what you did that upset him or her is that your partner's thoughts are now out in the open rather than stirring in a stew of resentment. To keep such openness in your relationship, it is important for you to let your partner know that you value such disclosure by saying something like, "I know it wasn't easy for you to tell me what I did that upset you, but I'm glad you told me. I needed to know what you were thinking."*

Such a statement by the therapist makes clear to the spouses the importance of keeping the process of communication/interaction alive (in spite of difficult content).

Ask "Honest Questions"

Good communication also involves asking honest questions. Dr. Charles Madsen of Florida State University noted that an **honest question** is a question that you ask someone with the intent of really wanting to know the answer. In effect, you don't have an answer that you want to hear and don't get mad at whatever the person answers. A **dishonest question** has a preset answer. Suppose one spouse asks another, "Do you want to go see my parents this weekend?" If the question is honest (the spouse really wants to know how their mate feels), the answer can be, "Are you kidding? Seeing your parents is the perfect way to screw up a weekend" and the spouse won't get mad. If the question is dishonest, and the partner says, "no," the spouse will be mad because a "yes" is what they really wanted to hear. Honest questions are important since they are a genuine attempt to find out what each partner thinks and feels. Other examples of honest and dishonest questions follow:

Question	Honest question if:	Dishonest question if:
"Suppose we have my office workers over for dinner Saturday night?"	Partner can say "no."	You get angry if ans. is "no."
"I'd like to buy a new car, that OK?"	Partner can say "no."	You get angry if ans. is "no."
"I'd like for us to move, that OK?"	Partner can say "no."	You get angry if ans. is "no."
"Can we try to get pregnant this fall?	Partner can say "no."	You get angry if ans. is "no."

The point is for spouses to give each other the respect of having a different opinion and not asking questions that have a preset answer.

Use Reflective Statements

Spouses should also be encouraged to use reflective statements. Good communication also involves the use of **reflective statements**. These are simply restatements of what each partner says to the other. For example, if he drones on about his boss at work, a good response from the wife might be to reflect what he's feeling: "You feel like you are being exploited and you are getting angry about it" communicates that the partner is "there" in terms of understanding the mate without being critical ("you are always complaining about something") or ignoring (saying nothing/being silent) the partner. Some examples of reflective statements follow:

Spouse says	Reflective statement	Judgmental response
"Your mother drives me up the wall."	"My mom upsets you."	"You hate my mom."
"Your brother drank too much."	"You think Tom overdid it."	"You never liked my brother."
"You spent too much on the wedding."	"You think I went overboard."	"You are a tightwad."
"I should have scheduled more time between flights. We're going to miss our connection."	"You're getting concerned about the tight connection time."	"You worry too much."

Use "I" Statements

When one spouse does something that upsets the other, the use of "I" statements rather than "you" statements is preferable. For example, rather than one spouse say, "You are always late and irresponsible" (which is a "you" statement), the spouse might, instead, say "I get upset when you are late and would feel better if you call me when you will be delayed." **"I" statements** focus on the speaker's feelings and the desirable future behavior rather than blaming the partner for being late.

Consider Measured Honesty

All relationships depend on some level of illusion. Each partner likes to feel loved, respected, and regarded as the unique soul mate. While spouses should communicate these true and real feelings to the partner, there are other thoughts each may have about the other that should be omitted, left out, and hidden: **measured honesty**. "You're getting a fat belly," "You're babbling on about nothing all the time drives me nuts," and "You wouldn't know how to be on time if it killed you," are likely hand grenades to start a shouting match/heated argument. The thoughts might best be kept to one's self since they are not likely to result in behavior change. Telling one's partner he or she has a beer belly isn't likely to get the partner to join the gym and being told that one is "babbling about nothing" is only going to hurt one's feelings. Sometimes, kindness is a quality of more value than blunt honesty.

Chapter 8

Case Histories: Spouses

*I love being married. It's so great to find that one special person you
want to annoy the rest of your life.*

Rita Rudner

The following represent some of our cases reflecting an array of marital issues. We present both successes and failures. And, to protect our clients, we have changed basic demographics so even the clients would not recognize themselves.

Case 1: Pornography Addiction

Couple

Wife complained that her husband was "addicted" to pornography as defined by his looking at Internet porn on the job and late at night (to which he would masturbate). The result of such viewing was that the husband was less interested in sex with his wife. The husband agreed that "pornography has become a problem." As an aside, he also felt that his wife was too involved with her parents (e.g. he was also upset with her over her behavior).

Feelings Presented

Wife felt hurt and unloved. She questioned her own sex appeal and desirability as a woman since her husband preferred to look at porno each night. Husband felt ambivalent — he enjoyed pornography but recognized it was a problem. Husband also felt his wife cared more about her parents than him.

Behavioral Referents

Wife felt betrayed due to husband preferring to look at pornography over wanting to have sex with her. Husband felt confused since he could not control his porno watching but felt he "should." He also felt his wife's being in constant (cell phone, text messaging) contact with her parents was abnormal.

Frequency of Behaviors

Wife reported husband declined sex three or four times weekly and watched porno on the computer seven nights a week for minimum of thirty minutes. Husband said wife talked with or text messaged her parents eight times daily and saw them five times a week, sometimes for hours on the weekend when they (the couple) could be together.

Behavioral Goal

Husband's goal was to decrease frequency of viewing pornography alone and to increase frequency of initiating sex with wife. Wife's goal was to decrease contact with her parents and increase the time she spent doing things with her husband.

Behavior Contracts

To reduce his need for watching porno, husband agreed to masturbate four times a day. Husband also agreed that he would no longer watch porno on the Internet and that he would give his wife the password on both his office and home computers so that she could verify no porn sites. Wife agreed to approach husband twice weekly for looking at porn together with sex to follow. Wife also agreed to cut in half the phone calls and visits with parents. Together the couple agreed to go out on a dinner date once a week, compliment each other twice a day, make no references to the past, and make no critical statements to each other.

Results

Husband masturbated as agreed and noted his reduced libido. He was able to restrict porno viewing to times with wife which was followed by sex (wife also enjoyed porn as a prelude to sex with her husband) with his wife. Wife did check computers of husband and, with one exception, found no porn watching. She also decreased the frequency of her parental contacts. At last session, couple reported there was no longer a need to meet since husband restricted his porn viewing to when he was with his wife, the frequency of their sex increased and the wife's contacts with her parents decreased.

Case 2: Office Affair

Spouse

Husband, seen alone, was ambivalent about whether to stay in his marriage of fifteen years. He had become attracted to a younger office mate and was excited about seeing and being with her. They had had sex once at a conference after which he questioned his commitment to his wife and two children.

Feelings Presented

Ambivalence about commitment to marriage. Bland feelings of love for the wife. In contrast, he had love/sexual excitement feelings in reference to the single young woman at work.

Behavioral Referents

"Water cooler time" with young woman at office and sex at a conference had created feelings of wanting to be with the office mate and to leave his wife. Absence of good sex with wife and enjoyable time with office mate resulted in being vulnerable to excitement/sex with young woman.

Frequency of Behaviors

Daily contact with the woman at work. Daily neutral to negative interaction with wife.

Behavioral Goal

Reduce ambivalence and decide if want to stay married.

Behavior Contracts

Husband agreed to stop water cooler conversations/flirting with young woman at office, no more sex with her, and to take wife out on a date once a week/initiate sex with wife once a week. Wife was also seen (she knew nothing about office woman) and agreed to more frequent time together, reduce negative statements to husband, and increased sex.

Results

Over a period of six months, husband gradually reduced time with office woman and increased time with wife. At last report, office woman had moved to new job and husband experienced renewed emotional and sexual relationship with his wife.

Case 3: Dual Affairs

Couple

Both spouses reported having an affair with a couple they mutually knew.

Feelings Presented

Feelings of not being loved/sexually desired by the spouse. Feeling jealous that spouse had had and enjoyed sex with friend's spouse.

Behavioral Referents

Sexual affair on the part of the respective spouses. Cognitions on the part of both spouses that "my spouse would really prefer to be with the other person."

Frequency of Behaviors

Both spouses reported constant (four times weekly) fights over the respective affairs — blaming each other with "how could you?" Each spouse also had intrusive thoughts of the spouse with the other person (three times weekly). Both denied wanting to be with the other person again.

Behavioral Goal

Stop constant bickering/accusations. Stop intrusive thoughts about affairs. Initiate/increase enjoyable sex between the partners.

Behavior Contracts

Content of behavior contracts was the same for both spouses.

	Mon.	Tues.	Wed.	Thurs.	Fri.	Sat.	Sun.
1. No mention of previous affair or person. If spouse brings it up, leave the room.	___	___	___	___	___	___	___
2. Out alone together once weekly for dinner.	___					___	___
3. Compliment spouse 2 times each day.	___	___	___	___	___	___	___
4. No negative statements to spouse.	___	___	___	___	___	___	___
5. Use "stop-think" technique for intrusive thoughts.	___	___	___	___	___	___	___

The **stop-think technique** involves yelling inside one's head "STOP" when an intrusive thought occurs and replacing it with a negative or alternative thought. In the case of reminiscing about a previous lover, the spouses were instructed to yell "STOP" in his or her head which would stop the romantic remembering of the affair person and replace the thought with "the person has Herpes" or "the person has a string of lovers and I was just one of them caught in the web" or shift to the joy of being "over with the anxiety of an affair" and keeping one's marriage and family together.

Results

Over a period of four months, the couple reported success in gradually moving beyond the explosiveness of the previous affairs to a focus on their own emotional and sexual relationship/marriage.

Case 4: Discrepancy over Frequency of Sex

Couple

The spouses loved each other but had very different sexual needs. The husband reported the need for sex a minimum of ten times a week which translated into more than twice a day at least five times a week. The wife reported a couple of times a week would be fine with her.

Feelings Presented

The wife felt anxious, inadequate, and pressured to satisfy what she viewed as unreasonable sexual demands made on her by her husband. Not only did she have a low libido, she had a young child which resulted in her being chronically exhausted. Her husband felt incessantly sexually deprived, frustrated, and resentful.

Behavioral Referents

Wife noted husband made it clear he wanted sex ten times a week. Husband noted wife turned him down eight times a week.

Frequency of Behaviors

See above.

Behavioral Goal

Reduce pressure on wife to have sex she did not want and reduce the level of sexual frustration husband experienced in reference to the low frequency of sex.

Behavior Contracts

The couple agreed to a compromise of sex six times a week — four times more than the wife wanted it and four times less than the husband wanted it. Wife also agreed that sexual desire was not a prerequisite for her engaging in sexual behavior, that she would be available to her husband sexually even though she did not have the sexual need herself. Wife loved her husband, wanted to please him and was OK with the idea of having sex with him when she did not feel horny. Husband was also accepting of idea that wife did not need to be "into having sex" on every occasion.

Husband also agreed to take "long shower" (masturbate) four times a week to reduce sexual pressure on wife. Wife would approach husband for sex three times and vice versa so each took some responsibility for sex occurring. Wife also had option of providing sex for husband in various ways — intercourse, oral sex, or hand job.

Results

Domino effect was illustrated by this couple. Once they discussed sexual issue and it became evident that they both wanted to resolve issue, husband became less angry about sex not occurring (and more flexible) and wife became more willing to ensure that sex occurred in the relationship (and more willing to initiate). The other issues in the relationship such as "messy house," "husband spends too much time on Blackberry," and "wife's part time job" all ceased to be issues.

Case 5: Medical Marriage

Couple

Successful busy physician, his wife, and three children presented a highly conflicted, estranged relationship.

Feelings Presented

Wife felt unappreciated in that she was "last on the list" in terms of her husband's priorities. Husband also felt unappreciated and neglected by intrusion of wife's career and her "girlfriends" taking priority over him.

Behavioral Referents

Wife's not feeling appreciated was based on her husband never telling her he appreciated her doing all the work with their three children and his never helping her at home with the chores. Husband's feelings that wife's career took precedence was based on his perception that she was "always out of town on business" and "always at the beach with her girlfriends."

Frequency of Behaviors

Husband acknowledged low frequency of verbal praise to wife. Wife's being out of town for business was twice every six months. Time with "girls at the beach" was one week in the summer and one weekend in the spring.

Behavioral Goal

Spouses identified feeling better about each other as their goal.

Behavior Contract for Husband	Mon.	Tues.	Wed.	Thurs.	Fri.	Sat.	Sun.
1. Notice and compliment wife twice per day for things she does for you and the children.	___	___	___	___	___	___	___
2. No negative statements to wife.	___	___	___	___	___	___	___
3. Meet wife for lunch once a week.	___	___	___	___	___	___	___
4. Out to dinner alone with wife once a week.	___	___	___	___	___	___	___
5. Put one child to bed each night.	___	___	___	___	___	___	___

Behavior Contract for Wife	Mon	Tues	Wed	Thurs	Fri	Sat	Sun
1. Notice and compliment husband twice per day for things he says or does which please you.	___	___	___	___	___	___	___
2. No negative statements to husband.	___	___	___	___	___	___	___
3. Meet husband for lunch once a week.	___	___	___	___	___	___	___
4. Out to dinner alone with husband once weekly.	___	___	___	___	___	___	___
5. Negotiate time with girlfriends with husband.	___	___	___	___	___	___	___

Results

Results were variable. When spouses engaged in behaviors, they reported the desired feeling changes. But they were not consistent. An argument could erupt which resulted in neither doing what he or she agreed to do for weeks. They would then return to therapy which resulted in a recommitment to "go back on the contracts."

Case 6: Alcoholism

Couple

Wife called for an appointment in regard to her husband's incessant drinking which resulted in his job loss and abuse. Since marriage therapy is NOT about treating alcoholism, therapist suggested wife see therapist who specializes in working with alcoholism with the goal of getting her husband into treatment. In the meantime, the wife might be seen by the alcohol counselor for "supportive therapy." Couple was not seen in our offices for marriage therapy since primary goal was for the husband to control his drinking, which he evidenced no interest in doing. There can be no productive marriage therapy with an alcoholic spouse since agreements between the alcoholic, spouse, and therapist are typically not kept. Since the result is no behavior change, there will be no concomitant change in feelings.

Case 7: Husband as Cross Dresser

Couple

The wife returned home unexpectedly from shopping to find her husband dressed in full female attire. He confided that he had been a cross dresser since adolescence and feared telling his wife of twelve years since she might "freak" and leave him.

Feelings Presented

The wife presented feelings of shock, disbelief, and a feeling of betrayal ("how could he keep this from me?"). The husband presented feelings of guilt for keeping this secret from his wife but acknowledged fear that she would leave him if he told her.

Behavioral Referents

The husband's hiding his fetish and his wife's reaction to his secret were the behavioral referents for his fear of abandonment and for her feelings of shock/disbelief/betrayal.

Frequency of Behaviors

The respective feelings permeated the relationship. Both spouses were in a state of panic.

Behavioral Goal

The wife's goal was to decide whether to leave her husband. The husband's goal was to get his wife to understand why he hid his cross-dressing and to get her to stay in the marriage.

Behavior Contracts

The wife agreed to read literature on cross-dressing (e.g. *My Husband is a Cross Dresser*), to talk with other wives of cross dressers, and to make a list of her husband's positives (good provider, supportive of wife's career, faithful, loving/attentive father, handyman, cooks dinner, etc.) and to read these when using the stop-think technique (described earlier). The husband agreed to not ask his wife any questions about how she was feeling but to give her time to process her discovery and to decide what to do.

Results

Over a period of weeks the wife came to accept her husband as a cross dresser. While she did not want to "see it" (he was to cross-dress when she was not home and to keep his women's clothes in another room) or to hear about it, she focused on the fact that he was a loving, faithful, supportive father and spouse. After seven years, they are still married and attend conventions of cross dressers together.

Case 8: Dual Career

Couple

The respective spouses had interesting and demanding careers and felt torn in regard to how to maintain their marriage when different opportunities were available in different states.

Feelings Presented

Ambivalence over whether to prioritize one's marriage over career.

Behavioral Referents

Each spouse was reinforced by their respective careers for spending eighty percent of their waking time in reference to their professions. Both were academics with each having opportunities for full-time tenure positions at different universities in different states.

Frequency of Behaviors

The couple had been separated by distance for three years but remained emotionally connected, faithful and loyal to each other.

Behavioral Goal

Resolve ambivalence.

Behavior Contracts

Weigh the respective pros and cons of moving closer to each other at different schools or both finding a smaller school where they could get jobs in different departments.

Results

Couple remained in their respective careers for twenty-five years at which time the wife got cancer and died. The couple remain one of the most successful long-distance dual-career marriages.

Case 9: Major Value Differences

Couple

Couple reported significant value differences over number of children. Husband wanted a "small family" as defined by two children. Wife wanted "large family" as defined by four or more. Wife also wanted to stay home with the children (not work outside the home) and wanted relationship focused on children. Husband wanted wife who earned an income and took trips with him on their sailboat. Indeed, he wanted wife to home school the children so the family could live on the sailboat.

Feelings Presented

Both spouses were unhappy to the point of considering separation.

Behavioral Referents

Wife was unhappy because she wanted husband to agree to more children and to stop pressuring her to take vacations alone with him. Husband was unhappy because he wanted an adult one-on-one relationship some of the time with his wife. He felt her demand for more children was unreasonable.

Frequency of Behaviors

Since the couple had their second child, they were unhappy with each other on a daily basis. They rarely did anything together as a couple.

Behavioral Goal

Reduce discrepancy in the relationship between what the respective spouses wanted.

Behavior Contracts

Contracts were not used with this couple.

Results

The partners maintained their respective positions. The wife wanted more children, to remain out of the work force and to have only family vacations. She thought the husband's idea to take their children out of public school and have her home school them on a sailboat was silly. The husband was adamant about no additional children, his wife earning an income, and would prefer to home school the children. The couple divorced.

Case 10: Loss of Love for Husband/Change of Sexual Orientation

Couple

Wife presented that she had fallen out of love with her husband and found herself attracted to a woman at work.

Feelings Presented

Wife felt guilty at her absence of love for her husband since she noted he was a good provider, faithful, and a good father to their three girls.

Behavioral Referents

Stimulus for wife's feelings was internal. Husband's behavior did not serve as "trigger." Again, wife valued husband as a partner and a father. "I could not ask for a better husband," she said.

Frequency of Behaviors

Wife had same-sex feelings since adolescence and had married to satisfy her parents' expectations and to have children. Now that her children were older, she no longer felt the need to keep up a social front and wanted to make a change.

Behavioral Goal

Wife was to examine the degree to which love feelings for her husband were necessary to continue her marriage and the degree to which she felt pulled/wanted to explore a same-sex relationship.

Behavior Contracts

Wife agreed to examine feelings between sessions. She was under no pressure to make decision but to follow her own timetable in terms of the future.

Results

Over a period of two years, the wife decided to leave the marriage and to begin living with a female partner. There was considerable difficulty making the transition for her, her husband, and her children. Nothing is easy about ending a relationship. But there are chronic problems in continuing a relationship where one feels partnered with the wrong sex.

Case 11: Only One Spouse Interested in Therapy

Spouse

Wife called and said that she and husband were in conflict but that he would not come in.

Feelings Presented

Wife was frustrated. She wanted an improved relationship but without her husband's participation, she felt hopeless.

Behavioral Referents

Husband's negative behavior of criticizing her, spending no time with her, and being unwilling to go to therapy with her were sources of her frustration.

Frequency of Behaviors

Wife reported daily critical remarks, no time alone with her for months, and recent refusal to go to therapy.

Behavioral Goal

Replace negative behavior of husband toward wife with pleasant behavior and increase time couple spends alone together.

Behavior Contracts

1. Wife was given self-addressed, stamped envelope to give to husband. Inside was a note from therapist alerting him that wife was being seen in therapy and he was asked to list three things his wife did that upset him and three things he wanted her to begin to do to please him.

2. Wife was asked to identify three things husband did that upset her and to conduct a functional analysis providing ABC data.

- A (Antecedent) — what was the stimulus or antecedent or thing or event which immediately happened before her husband engaged in the behavior she did not like? For example, if he criticized her, when exactly did he do this — after two bottles of beer, when he came in from work, when he stepped on her clothes in the bedroom, etc.?
- B (Behavior) — what behavior did her husband engage in which upset her? Did he yell at her, call her names, criticize her, etc.?
- C (Consequence) — what consequence followed the negative behavior? If he criticized her, what did she do when he did so or what was the consequence of his criticizing her in terms of her behavior? Did she cry, leave the room, criticize him back . . . what was the consequence?

Results

Husband did not mail in sheet identifying what he wanted his wife to do. Therapist called husband and asked if he would be willing to come in for one session, alone, and that his wife would pay. Goal was for him to identify what his wife could do to make his life better — therapist agreed there would be no focus on his behavior or what she wanted him to do. Husband came in and said that he and his wife "argued all the time" and that he was unsure if he wanted to remain married. Therapist expressed appreciation for the husband coming to the session and made no demands on him.

Wife's records revealed that she inadvertently was reinforcing her husband's being argumentative by having sex with him after a big argument. She was asked to look down and away when he would make negative statements to her or try to start an argument with her. She was to only have sex with him on those days he was nice to her.

Couple did not improve and dropped out of therapy.

Case 12: Spouse Depressed in Wake of Divorce

Spouse

Wife called to report that she was unable to adjust to end of marriage. She had lost weight, was not sleeping, not eating, and chronically crying.

Feelings Presented

Utter despair.

Behavioral Referents

End of marriage.

Frequency of Behaviors

Wife was asked to identify when she felt sad/depressed at a level of eight on a ten-point scale and to write down the accompanying thoughts. Results revealed high daily frequency of negative self-referent statements — "I am a failure," "I let a good man go," "I should never have hurt him," "No one will ever love me again," "I am damaged goods," and "My life is over without him." Wife also drank three to six glasses of wine every afternoon/evening and spent all of her time alone.

Behavioral Goal

Goal was to decrease negative self-referent statements with positive self-referent statements, to limit drinking to one glass of wine with dinner, and to initiate time with friends three nights a week. The wife was also told that adjustment to a divorce is a gradual process and that most individuals take from twelve to eighteen months to complete the process.

Behavior Contracts

The **stop-think technique** was described whereby she would think "stop" each time she had a negative self-referent statement such as 'I am a failure and I can never recover" and to replace the thought with a positive self-referent statement such as "I made a mistake but everyone does; I will recover and move on."

The wife also agreed to limit her alcohol intake to one glass of wine with dinner and to keep a record of the amount of alcohol she consumed.

The wife also agreed to set up time to be with friends on three evenings a week.

Results

Over a twelve-month period, the wife reported feeling less depressed. Her records also revealed a gradual reduction/elimination of negative self-referent statements and a replacement of positive self-referent statements. Her social network also improved as defined by her spending time with her girlfriends at least twice a week. She also had begun to date one of the friends of one of her girlfriends.

Case 13: One Spouse Neglecting Another*

John and Sally are both thirty-four years old and have been married for four years. John is an internist with a busy practice and Sally is a registered dietician. She is primarily a stay-at-home mom, but who does some patient counseling when her husband has a particularly difficult patient. At issue is the fact that John's father was a surgeon who tended to see any contact with the family during work hours as being an intrusion and disruption in trying to see patients. John seems to be falling into his father's pattern and acting as if his wife's attempts to say hello to him between patients was a bother. This pattern of behavior has led to arguments averaging four times a week.

Behavioral Goal

New behaviors for John to engage in were identified:

1. Increase John's responding to Sally positively during the day.

2. Decrease Sally's negative self talk and critical remarks to John regarding her feeling that John places all other obligations ahead of interactions with her.

Strategy

John was instructed that each time he saw his wife for the first time that day in the office, he would divert into the room she was, give her a big hug, tell her he loved her and ask how she was. Sally was to respond to his approach with a smile, tell him she appreciated his time, and was to allow him to return to work without feeling she was abandoned. John was asked to track the amount of time per day that these interactions took.

---

* Cases 13 and 14 have been contributed by Robert Sammons, MD, Ph.D., a psychiatrist in Grand Junction, Colo. Dr. Sammons specializes in behavioral medicine.

Outcome

The couple returned two weeks later with John saying he did not keep track of the time. However, he said the time spent hugging his wife and having a brief conversation with her was negligible in terms of the day. And the reinforcement John received from his actions, in terms of increased responsiveness on Sally's part and the decreased number of arguments, was extremely reinforcing and caused him to continue the behavior.

When the couple was seen at three- and six-month follow-up visits, the positive behavior pattern they had begun had continued. John was surprised at the small amount of time it actually took to let his wife know he cared about her, was happy to see her, and wished he had more time when he didn't. Sally was appreciative of John disrupting his day, if only for a few moments, to recognize she was in the office, and responding to her in a positive way. She said this significantly improved the way she felt about John.

Case 14: Spouse's Depression Affects the Family

Gary, Linda, and their two children, ages ten and fourteen, were being seen for family therapy. Gary had been injured on an oil rig, was on Workers' Compensation and was only receiving a portion of his original pay. His chronic pain and the financial difficulties had resulted in his being depressed. He, Linda, and the children were fighting frequently and everyone seemed unhappy with everyone else. Because of Gary's pain and lack of money, the family was able to go out less frequently. By going out less frequently, Gary was becoming more depressed and the family was becoming increasingly irritable. They lived in a rural community of approximately 50,000 people.

Behavioral Goal

The goal of therapy was to reduce Gary's depression by increasing the reinforcement he was experiencing.

Intervention

The local newspaper had a Friday supplement called "Out & About." In this supplement, there was a listing of the following week's activities including sections on sports, music, theater, dance, art, museums, and miscellaneous.

Gary and Linda were asked to get an "Out & About" section of the newspaper and circle all activities which were of interest to them and/or their children, regardless of time, location, or cost. After the activities had been circled, they were asked to go through the list a second time and check the activities which they could afford, were close in location, and where the timing would work. As a family they were asked to choose two activities per week to attend, with one preference being one chosen by the parents and one by the children.

Outcome

The family was seen again in two weeks and had gone to four events. The parents had chosen a free outdoor concert by The Centennial Band and a free lecture at the local college on ancient aboriginal music. The children had chosen to attend a parade and a Harry Potter-themed activity at the local library. The family enjoyed each of these activities and was looking forward to future activities.

Gary reported that the activities were not as enjoyable as they had been when he had not been in pain. He was asked to make a comparison between attending the events or staying home, doing nothing and being in pain. He was instructed not to compare the new activities to the best time he had doing these activities in the past, as he would always be disappointed. Gary found this change in cognitive referents helpful. The couple was seen again in a month and reported that Gary's depression had lifted, that the couple and kids were less irritated with each other, that they had less of a sense of helplessness, and were more hopeful about their difficult situation.

Comment

Depression has many causes, but from a behavioral perspective, loss of reinforcement and loss of reinforcer effectiveness will always exacerbate or cause depression. When a spouse is injured, there is generally a decrease in income and the effect on the family is to stay home where the unhappiness and bickering fester and increase.

As a person becomes depressed, he or she experiences a lack of energy, a lack of motivation to do anything, and a lack of enjoyment in previously enjoyable activities. As such, when they engage in an activity, it is perceived as not being as enjoyable as it had been in the past, which has the effect of further reducing his or her motivation to engage in the activities. Eventually some spouses stop engaging in any outside activities, which has the consequence of depriving them of an array of reinforcers when they stay at home. This is analogous to being under house arrest and, when this concept is explained, people often recognize the consequence of isolation at home and the negative consequence on their depression.

When spouses are depressed, they can often have a sense of helplessness and may not be aware of the options that are available to them. Having a structured process, such as a list of events in a weekly calendar or a weekly newspaper, allows them to evaluate the various opportunities that are available to them and to pick and choose an activity that may be enjoyable. Having the family members circle every event that would be enjoyable, whether they can attend it or not, increases their awareness that there are enjoyable activities available in the community, even though they may not all be affordable or obtainable. Having the family then check the items they can afford and arrange to attend demonstrates the variety of options to sitting at home and being depressed. It is often easier to choose from a list than it is for a depressed person to think of something to do without having any cues.

By getting out of the house and attending activities there is a breaking of the depressive cycle of staying home, the chance of increased exposure to reinforcers outside the home, and the reality of having a pleasant experience. One cannot be both enjoying activities outside the home and be depressed at the same time. Once the cycle is broken, the spouses and children repeat the reinforcing activities.

Case 15: Spouse's Difficult Adjustment to Birth of Baby*

Couple

White collar twenty-nine-year-old male was seen with his twenty-eight-year-old wife in reference to husband's difficulty adjusting to fatherhood. Sound of crying baby, wife's exhaustion, and end of couple/romance time as he viewed it resulted in deep marital unhappiness on the part of the father. Wife was distraught that husband reacted negatively to birth of their baby and beside herself in regard to what to do.

* Case History 15 was contributed by Louise Sammons, Doctorate in Education and an R.N. and former officer in North Carolina Marriage and Family Therapy Association. Dr. Sammons is in private practice in Grand Junction, Colo.

Intervention

Father was informed that males differ in reaction to fatherhood but that most find enjoyment in parenthood when child begins to talk and walk. In the meantime, father was encouraged to take an active role in taking care of child via feeding and bathing. Couple was also instructed to get baby sitter and to go out alone to renew their marital relationship.

Outcome: Father's attitude toward the baby and the couple's relationship slowly improved over a two-year period. At year three, wife insisted on having another child which husband was against.

The couple dropped out of therapy but ended up having a second child and eventually getting a divorce. Father ended up enjoying and having good relationships with both children.

Chapter 9

Family Therapy Forms

Family Inventory*

Purpose of Family Inventory

The purpose of the Family Inventory is to obtain a comprehensive picture of your family. By answering these questions as completely and as accurately as you can, you will facilitate your family therapy program. You are requested to answer these questions on your own time instead of using time in therapy. Please complete the Family Inventory with the other parent or adult who is a meaningful part of your child's life. It is understandable that you might be concerned about what happens to the Family Inventory. Because much or all of this information is highly personal, your inventory is strictly confidential. No outsider is permitted to see your Inventory without your permission.

I. GENERAL

Name_____

Address _____

Email Address _____

Telephone Numbers _____

Mother: Age _____ Occupation _____ Father: Age _____ Occupation _____

By whom were you referred? _____

Circle the appropriate answer: Married   Separated   Divorced   Widowed   Never married

Is this your: First marriage?   Second marriage?   Third marriage?   Other?

Names and ages of your children: Name   Age   Child of which marriage?

　　　　　　　　　　　　　　1._____

　　　　　　　　　　　　　　2._____

　　　　　　　　　　　　　　3._____

　　　　　　　　　　　　　　4._____

Are you currently living with your spouse?   Yes _____   No _____

If you are not living with your spouse, how long have you been separated/divorced? _____

If you are divorced:

Which parent has legal physical custody?_____

What is the visitation agreement with the other parent?_____

_____

_____

What is your relationship with your former spouse?   Best buddies   Civil   At war

Level of involvement other parent has with children?   Very little   Moderate   Extensive

II. CLINICAL

A. Circle the following words and phrases which apply to you:

A "nobody," "life is empty," a "somebody," "life is fun," stupid, bright, incompetent, competent, naïve, sophisticated, guilty, at peace with self, horrible thoughts, pleasant thoughts, unpleasant thoughts, full of hate, full of love, anxious, panicky, relaxed, cowardly, confident, unassertive, assertive, aggressive, friendly, ugly, beautiful, deformed, shapely, attractive, unattractive, pleasant, repulsive, depressed, happy, lonely, wanted, needed, unloved, loved, misunderstood, bored, active, restless, confused, full of pleasant thoughts about past events, worthwhile, sympathetic, intelligent, considerate.

Prescription drugs I am taking are: 1. _____   2. _____   3. _____

III. PROBLEM AREAS WITH CHILD

Circle each problem area you are having with your child. If more than one child, put a square around the number in reference to your youngest child and a circle around the words for the other child of concern.

A. BEDTIME   B. EATING

1. Won't sleep alone   1. What child eats

2. Bed wetting   2. Amount child eats

3. Won't go to bed   3. Messy eater

4. Won't stay in bed   4. Throws food

5. Won't go to sleep   5. Plays with food

6. Gets up several times   6. Talks with mouth open

C. INTERACTION WITH SIBLING

   1. Picks fight with

   2. Hurts sibling

   3. Jealous of sibling

   4. Steals clothes

   5. Bullies

E. TOILETING

   1. Difficulty initiating

   2. Handles feces

G. DESTRUCTIVE

   1. Destroys school property

   2. Destroys parents' property

I. SCHOOL

   1. Poor grades

   2. Does not study

   OTHER? _____

D. SOCIAL RELATIONSHIPS

   1. No friends

   2. Hurts friends

   3. Unacceptable friends

   4. Impolite to friends

   5. Critical of friends

F. COMPLIANCE

   1. Does not do as asked

   2. Talks back to parents

H. PHYSICAL PROBLEMS

   1. Overweight

   2. Developmentally delayed

J. GRANDPARENTS

   1. Competes with parents

   2. Too intrusive

IV. PRIORITY

What behavior with which child would you like to work on first? _____

_____

_____

V. BEHAVIORAL SNAPSHOT

1. What behaviors does your child engage in that please you? _____

_____

_____

2. What behaviors do you want your child to increase or develop?_____

_____

_____

3. What are the top three things your child likes to do? (e.g. play video games, swim, etc.) _____

_____

_____

4. Please add any information which you feel may aid your therapist in understanding you and your family. Write any questions you have or identify any issues you would like to discuss.

_____

_____

_____

—End of Family Inventory—

Example of Completed Behavior Contract for Child

Mary will *do homework* beginning *Monday at 4:15 PM* for *Monday through Friday*. For doing so, she will have earned the privilege *to watch TV after dinner* and for not doing so, will forfeit the reward.

Other behaviors for *Mary* to engage in:

Use soft voice in house

Take off shoes after entering house

Say "please" and "thank you"

Play cooperatively with sibling

Other rewards for desirable behavior:

Play video games

Use phone

Dessert after dinner

Have friend over to spend the night

Blank Behavior Contract for Child

_____ (name of child) will _____ (desirable behavior) beginning

_____ (day of week) for _____ (days of week). For doing so, the child will

have earned the privilege to _____ (reward) and for not doing so, will forfeit the reward.

Other behaviors to engage in:

2. _____

3. _____

4. _____

5. _____

Other rewards for desirable behavior:

2. _____

3. _____

4. _____

5. _____

Example of Completed Frequency Chart for Child

Mary — daughter   Date: *Dec 1–7*

Mom — record keeper

	Days of Week						
Behaviors to Begin	Mon.	Tues.	Wed.	Thurs.	Fri.	Sat.	Sun
1. *Homework*	yes	yes	yes	yes	yes	na	na
2. *Use soft voice in house*	no	yes	yes	no	yes	yes	no
3. *Take off shoes after entering house*	yes	yes	yes	no	no	yes	no
4. *Say "please" and "thank you"*	yes	yes	yes	yes	yes	no	yes
5. *Play cooperatively with sibling*	yes	yes	no	yes	yes	no	yes

Blank Child Frequency Chart

_____ (Name of Child)   Date: _____

_____ (Name of Parent Keeping Records)

	Days of Week						
Behaviors to begin	Mon.	Tues.	Wed.	Thurs.	Fri.	Sat.	Sun.
1. _____	—	—	—	—	—	—	—
2. _____	—	—	—	—	—	—	—
3. _____	—	—	—	—	—	—	—
4. _____	—	—	—	—	—	—	—
5. _____	—	—	—	—	—	—	—

Example of Completed Agreement with Parents

Mary and John (parents of Mark) agree to *make two positive statements to Mark each day about something he did that pleased them* (desirable behavior) and to follow through with positive consequences if the desired behavior occurs and with negative consequences if the behavior does not occur.

		Days of Week					
New behaviors for parents	Mon.	Tues.	Wed.	Thurs.	Fri.	Sat.	Sun
	Mary	Mary	Mary		Mary		Mary
1. *Make two positive statements to Mark*	___	John	John	___	___	___	___
	Mary	Mary	Mary	Mary	Mary	Mary	
2. *Follow through with positive consequence*	John	___	___	John	___	___	___
3. *Follow through with negative consequence*	John	___	___	___	John	___	___

(This contract shows that the first week Mary made two positive statements to Mark five days; John did so only twice. Mary also followed through with positive consequence five of seven days; John twice. John followed with negative consequence twice; Mary none at all.)

Blank Agreement with Parents

_____ (parents of child) agree to _____ (desirable behavior) and to follow through with positive consequences if the desired behavior occurs and with negative consequences if the behavior does not occur.

		Days of Week					
New behaviors for parents	Mon.	Tues.	Wed.	Thurs.	Fri.	Sat.	Sun.
1. _____	___	___	___	___	___	___	___
2. _____	___	___	___	___	___	___	___
3. _____	___	___	___	___	___	___	___

Example of Completed Time Frequency Chart

Child: Jill   Put the letter of the code in the box at the time it occurs.
Record keeper: Mom or Dad   Therapist will ask for record chart each session.
Behavior: Talking back   An empty box means no behavior occurred.
Week of: 5/5/08–5/12/08   B = talking back

	Mon.	Tues.	Wed.	Thurs.	Fri.	Sat.	Sun.
6:00 AM							
7:00 AM							
8:00 AM	B			B		B	B
9:00 AM		B	B			B	B
10:00 AM							
11:00 AM							
12:00 PM							
1:00 PM							
2:00 PM							
3:00 PM							
4:00 PM							
5:00 PM							
6:00 PM	B	B			B	B	
7:00 PM			B	B			B
8:00 PM							
9:00 PM							
10:00 PM							
11:00 PM							
12:00 AM							

Example of Blank Time Frequency Chart

Child: _____   Put the letter of the code in the box at the time it occurs.
Record keeper: _____   Therapist will ask for record chart each session.
Behavior: _____   An empty box means no behavior occurred.
Week of: _____   B =

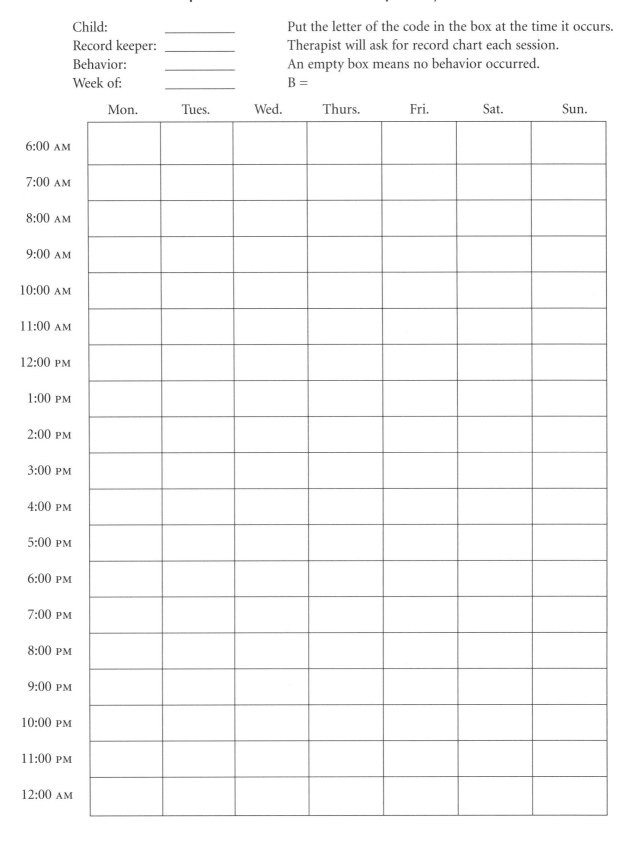

	Mon.	Tues.	Wed.	Thurs.	Fri.	Sat.	Sun.
6:00 AM							
7:00 AM							
8:00 AM							
9:00 AM							
10:00 AM							
11:00 AM							
12:00 PM							
1:00 PM							
2:00 PM							
3:00 PM							
4:00 PM							
5:00 PM							
6:00 PM							
7:00 PM							
8:00 PM							
9:00 PM							
10:00 PM							
11:00 PM							
12:00 AM							

Example of Completed ABC Form

Date: 2-24-08   Time of Day: 4:30 PM

1. What behavior did you see?

   __ fighting   __ running away   __ breaks things   X tantrum

   __ refusing to follow rules (describe)_____

   __ aggression (describe) _____

   __ other _____

2. What was going on when the behavior occurred?

   __ school work (what?) _____

   X asked to do something (what? *Sit down and eat lunch*).

   __ asked not to do something (what?)_____

   __ told to stop doing something (what?)_____

3. Who was around when the behavior started?

   __ mom   __ dad   __ sister   __ brother   __ teacher   __ classmates   X people in store

   __ other _____

4. Where was he/she when the behavior started?

   __ outside   __ classroom   __ kitchen   __ bedroom   __ living room   __ in car

   __ grocery store   X shopping   __ restaurant

   __ other (where?) _____

   __ other (where?) _____

5. What happened after the behavior occurred?

   __ taken from the room   __ spanked   __ sat in time out   X spoken to   __ left alone   __ grounded

Example of Blank ABC Form*

Date: _____   Time of Day: _____

1. What behavior did you see?

    __ fighting   __ running away   __ breaks things   __ tantrum

    __ refusing to follow rules (describe)_____

    __ aggression (describe) _____

    __ other _____

2. What was going on when the behavior occurred?

    __ school work (what?) _____

    __ asked to do something (what?) _____

    __ asked not to do something (what?)_____

    __ told to stop doing something (what?)_____

3. Who was around when the behavior started?

    __ mom   __ dad   __ sister   __ brother   __ teacher   __ classmates   __ people in store

    __ other _____

4. Where was he/she when the behavior started?

    __ outside   __ classroom   __ kitchen   __ bedroom   __ living room   __ in car

    __ grocery store   __ shopping   __ restaurant

    __ other (where?) _____

    __ other (where?) _____

5. What happened after the behavior occurred?

    __ taken from the room   __ spanked   __ sat in time out   __ spoken to   __ left alone   __ grounded

Chapter 10

Marriage Therapy Forms

Marriage Inventory*

Purpose of Marriage Inventory

The purpose of the Marriage Inventory is to obtain a comprehensive picture of you and your marriage. By answering these questions as completely and as accurately as you can, you will facilitate your therapy program. You are requested to answer these questions on your own time instead of using time in therapy. Each spouse is to complete the Inventory. Please complete the Inventory when you are alone and do not discuss your answers with your spouse. It is understandable that you might be concerned about what happens to the Marriage Inventory. Because much or all of this information is highly personal, your inventory is strictly confidential. No outsider is permitted to see your Inventory without your permission.

1. GENERAL

Name _____

Address _____

Email Address _____

Telephone Numbers _____

Age _____ Occupation _____

By whom were you referred? _____

How long have you been married?_____ Is this your first marriage? Yes _____ No _____

If second marriage, what is interval between first and second marriage? _____

If third marriage, what is interval between second and third marriage?_____

Names and ages of your children: Name   Age   Child of which marriage?

1._____

2._____

3._____

4._____

Are you currently living with your spouse?   Yes ____   No ____

If you are not living with your spouse, how long have you been separated/divorced? _____

Have you ever been separated from your spouse?   Yes ____   No ____

2. CLINICAL

A. Circle the following words and phrases which apply to you:

A "nobody," "life is empty," a "somebody," "life is fun," stupid, bright, incompetent, competent, naïve,

sophisticated, guilty, at peace with self, horrible thoughts, pleasant thoughts, unpleasant thoughts,

full of hate, full of love, anxious, panicky, relaxed, cowardly, confident, unassertive, assertive,

aggressive, friendly, ugly, beautiful, deformed, shapely, attractive, unattractive, pleasant, repulsive,

depressed, happy, lonely, wanted, needed, unloved, loved, misunderstood, bored, active, restless,

confused, full of pleasant thoughts about past events, worthwhile, sympathetic, intelligent, considerate

Prescription drugs I am taking are: 1. _____   2. _____   3. _____

B. Circle the following which apply to you:

Headaches, dizziness, in love, stomach trouble, chronic fatigue, nightmares, feel loved, elated,

feel panicky, depressed, suicidal ideas, unable to relax, overly ambitious, OCD,

don't like weekends/vacations, inferiority feelings, can't make friends, satisfied, can't keep a job,

happy, fainting spells, take drugs, no appetite, obsessive, can't make decisions, drunk more than

twelve times a year, insomnia, unable to have a good time, concentration difficulties, tremors

3. PROBLEM AREAS IN MARRIAGE

Circle each problem area you are having in your marriage. Include additional information on the last page of the Marriage Inventory if necessary.

A. SEX   B. COMMUNICATION

1. Lack of sexual desire   1. Don't feel close to spouse

SEX *continued*

  2. Infrequent or no orgasm

  3. Pain during intercourse

  4. Vagina too tight for penetration

  5. Ejaculate too soon

  6. Difficulty maintaining erection

  7. No ejaculation

  8. Disagreement over how sex occurs

    a. Too little foreplay

    b. Spouse crude in approach

    c. Oral sex

    d. Anal sex

    e. Positions

    f. Other

  9. Frequency of Intercourse

10. Disagreement over when sex occurs

11. Extramarital affair

12. Internet porno

C. MONEY

1. Too little money

2. Wife's job

3. Husband's job

4. Husband doesn't trust wife with money

5. Wife doesn't trust husband with money

6. Gambling

7. Conflict over who buys what

8. Borrowing

9. Excessive debts

COMMUNICATION *continued*

  2. Rarely alone with spouse

  3. Spouse complains/criticizes

  4. Don't love spouse

  5. Spouse doesn't love me

  6. Spouse is impatient and irritable

  7. We spend too little time communicating

  8. Nothing to talk about

  9. Intellectual gaps

10. Topic or type of conversation

11. Spouse is unhappy and depressed

12. We argue, bicker, and pick at each other

13. Arguing which ends in abuse/violence

D. PARENTS AND IN-LAWS

1. Incessant talking on phone to parents/inilaws

2. How often parents/in-laws visit

3. How often to visit parents/in-laws

4. Borrowing money from parents/in-laws

5. Dislike of parents/in-laws

6. Parents/in-laws dislike spouse

7. Parents/in-laws try to run spouse's life

8. Parents/in-laws living with couple

9. Supporting parents/in-laws

E. RELIGION

1. Which church to attend

2. Wife too devout

3. Husband too devout

4. Wife not devout enough

5. Husband not devout enough

6. Religion to rear children in

7. How much money to give to church

8. Observance of religious holidays

9. Disagreement over religious rituals (e.g. circumcision)

10. Breaking of vows

G. FRIENDS

1. Too few friends

2. Too many friends

3. Different friends

4. Confidences to friends

5. Friends over for dinner not often enough

6. Friends over for dinner too often

7. Don't like partner's friends

I. CHILDREN

1. Discipline of children

2. Care of children

3. Time with children

4. Number of children

5. Spacing of children

6. Infertility

7. Whether or not to adopt

F. RECREATION

1. No sharing of leisure time

2. Spouse takes separate vacations

3. Competition between egos in sports

4. Amount of $ to be spent on vacations

5. Spouse doesn't like family vacations

6. Spouse won't vacation if kids not along

7. Where to spend vacations

8. Spouse won't take time for vacation

9. Disagreement over what is fun

10. Spouse plays video games too much

H. ALCOHOL/DRUGS

1. Spouse drinks too much

2. Marijuana, cocaine, other drugs

3. Spouse takes too many pills

4. Amount of money spent on alcohol

5. Flirting resulting from too much alcohol

6. Alcohol use as bad model for children

7. Violence resulting from too much alcohol

CHILDREN *continued*

8. Rivalry for children's love

9. Activities children should be involved in

10. Sex education for children

11. Temper tantrums of children

12. Child abuse

13. Unwanted pregnancy

14. Step-children

IV. PRIORITY

What specifically would you like to work on first? Rank the problems in the order that you would like to deal with them. _____

_____

V. BEHAVIORAL SNAPSHOT

1. What behaviors do you engage in that please your spouse?_____

_____

2. What behaviors do you want to increase or develop in your self?_____

_____

3. What behaviors does your spouse engage in that please you?

_____

4. What behaviors do you want your spouse to increase or develop?

_____

5. Please add any information which you feel may aid your therapist in understanding you, your spouse, and/or your relationship. Write any questions you have or identify any issues you would like to discuss.

_____

_____

_____

— End of Marriage Inventory —

Example of Completed Behavior Contract for Husband

Chet (Name of Husband)   Date: Week of *June 8–14*

Behaviors husband agrees to engage in	Days of Week						
	Mon.	Tues.	Wed.	Thurs.	Fri.	Sat.	Sun
1. *Be on time or call Maria if late*	yes	yes	yes	na	yes	na	na
2. *Compliment Maria twice each day*	yes	yes	yes	yes	yes	yes	yes
3. *No negative statements to Maria*	no	no	yes	yes	yes	no	yes
4. *Set up "date" on Wed. for Sat. with Maria*	na	na	yes	na	na	no	na
5. *Go out on a "date" Sat. night with Maria*	na	na	na	na	na	yes	na

Blank Behavior Contract for Husband

_____ (Name of Husband) Date: _____

Days of Week

Behaviors husband agrees to engage in	Mon.	Tues.	Wed.	Thurs.	Fri.	Sat.	Sun
1. _____	—	—	—	—	—	—	—
2. _____	—	—	—	—	—	—	—
3. _____	—	—	—	—	—	—	—
4. _____	—	—	—	—	—	—	—
5. _____	—	—	—	—	—	—	—

Example of Completed Behavior Contract for Wife

Maria (Name of Wife)   Date: Week of *June 8–14*

Days of Week

Behaviors wife agrees to engage in	Mon.	Tues.	Wed.	Thurs.	Fri.	Sat.	Sun
1. *Initiate sex twice a week*	—	—	—	—	—	yes	yes
2. *Compliment Chet twice each day*	no	no	yes	no	yes	yes	no
3. *No negative statements to Chet*	yes	no	yes	no	no	yes	yes
4. *Negotiate time/place for date with Chet*	na	na	yes	na	na	na	na
5. *Out alone with Chet on a date Sat. night*	na	na	na	na	na	yes	na

Blank Behavior Contract for Wife

_____ (Name of Wife)   Date: _____

	Days of Week						
Behaviors wife agrees to engage in	Mon.	Tues.	Wed.	Thurs.	Fri.	Sat.	Sun
1. _____	___	___	___	___	___	___	___
2. _____	___	___	___	___	___	___	___
3. _____	___	___	___	___	___	___	___
4. _____	___	___	___	___	___	___	___
5. _____	___	___	___	___	___	___	___

Epilogue

Why Family Behavioral Therapy Does Not Work

Behavioral family therapy does not work for precisely the same reason that it does work. When parents do not reward the positive behavior of their children or punish negative behavior, the result is noncompliant, impolite, surly, and rebellious children. The great American tragedy is that the philosophy of individualism (unknown to traditional Eastern families) translates into parents doing their own thing (in both work and recreation) and relegating their children to day care centers, baby sitters, and TV. Parents who do not see gains in family therapy discover that effective parenting is time-intensive work and drop the ball.

The message for family therapists is to make therapy as positive an experience as possible, from reinforcing parents for being on time the first session, to record keeping, to following through with appropriate consequences for their children's behavior. In so doing, everyone wins. The parents relish in their children maturing into productive adulthood, society has a new generation of members who work and care about each other, and family therapists feel pride in a job well done.

Index